STONY CREEK DINER

DINER

A novel

Phyllis — Join me for coffee and muffins at my favorite diner. Love, Sharon

SHARON ALLEN

ISBN:-13: 978-1478376194
ISBN –10: 1478376198

Printed in the United States of America

Other Works by Sharon Allen

Novels:

Detours of the Heart

Short Stories:

For the Love of Scott

Published in
Journeys - An Anthology of Short Stories
A book written by The Village Writers

For more information about Sharon visit her website,
www.sharonallenauthor.com

DEDICATION

I dedicate this book to Linda Wilcox, my bestie from Montana. She was my confidant, my shoulder to cry on when I needed one, and she encouraged me to stand up for myself when it was difficult to do so. We are forever friends.

Montana holds a special place in my heart. The sky is bigger and bluer than any place I know of, the mountains are majestic and ever changing, and the people are down to earth and welcoming. I will be back!

ACKNOWLEDGEMENTS

Many thanks to Lorraine Harris, Pat Laplame, Julie McGlone, Christie Seiler Boeke, Peggy Hatfield, Nancy Snyder and Angela Hauzer, members of The Write Corner. They have laughed with me and cried with me throughout the writing of this book. They've encouraged me and critiqued my work (making a face here) with love and support. You girls are the best!
These women are published authors. Their books can be purchased on Amazon, Kindle, and Nook.

Many thanks and love to my husband who encourages me to do whatever it is I think I can do. It keeps me out of his hair.
Thanks to my children who are proud of me for attempting to be an author… my lifelong dream.
And to all my friends who love me just because I'm me.

Thanks to Marie Tennant who so graciously edited this book.

CHAPTER ONE

THIRTY-EIGHT YEAR OLD Meredith Parker Banning slipped through the side door of the gymnasium. Hoping to remain unnoticed, she stood with her back against the wall until her eyes became accustomed to the dimly lit room. *Stand by Your Man* was blasting over the sound system.

Butterflies had taken up residence in her stomach and were dancing to the beat of the music. Beads of perspiration dampened her armpits. Her knees threatened to buckle and for a fleeting moment she was afraid she might pass out.

"Come on, Meredith!" she chastised herself. "Suck it up. You've been waiting twenty years for this night."

Twenty years ago, Meredith left Buffalo High School and her hometown of Stony Creek, Montana. Vowing never to return, she kept her word until a recent family crisis made it impossible for her to stay away.

She had to admit that being back in the school scared her to death. Class reunion was as good a time as any to put her old demons to rest.

Twisted crepe paper streamers of green and white, the school's colors, along with helium-filled balloons decorated the gym for the occasion. A silver-mirrored ball rotated slowly from the ceiling while a disc jockey spun records from a makeshift stage. A handful of couples were dancing. Reminiscent of her high school days, she noticed the guys congregating in one corner of the gym and the girls in another.

Apparently, the common attire for social functions in Stony Creek was jeans, shirts, cowboy boots and hats for the men, denim skirts and blouses for the women. She should have remembered that. She felt like an overdressed buffoon in her black silk just-above-the knee-length dress and black pumps, making her stick out like a sore thumb, just like years ago. *Oh, and let's not forget the stupid, little black beaded purse in my hand.*

Looking at the empty tables scattered around the room her anxiety heightened. Should she stay or should she turn and slither out the way she came in, hoping no one would see her? *No freakin' way! I will not give in to the fears that have tortured me all of my life.*

Mustering up her courage, she pushed away from the wall that had been holding her up. Swallowing hard, she chewed on her lower lip, and with head held high, made her way across the gym floor. Feeling every eye in the room was on her, she quickly sat down at the first table she reached. Palms moist with perspiration and breathing unsteady she wondered, *Why am I putting myself through this? These people mean nothing to me and they never did.*

The women, chattering among themselves, didn't seem to notice Meredith's arrival although several of the men admiringly looked her way. One of them edged his way out of the crowd and swaggered over to her, taking a swig off his beer.

"Hi." He smiled, full of confidence and tipped his hat to her. Brazenly he leaned closer, eyeing her from head to toe. Liking what he saw he grinned and nodded his head.

Meredith recognized an older Taylor Boone with half a halo of hair and the top of his head virtually bald. His face sported a day's growth of beard and a beer belly fell over the belt of his jeans. *He sure isn't all that anymore,* she noted.

Taylor Boone, football jock and the most popular boy in school, had been her self-appointed tormentor throughout her school years. As mean as he was to her, Meredith felt he was the cutest boy in school and harbored a secret crush. All that changed the night of the senior prom.

The Boone family bragged to everyone within earshot that they were direct descendants of Daniel Boone. It made them feel entitled and they treated most people with disregard. In all actuality, they were nothing more than poor white trash. Taylor, who was the worst of the bunch, made Meredith's life pure hell. He was a bully and enjoyed his so-called privilege. Her stomach tightened into a knot as he pulled out a chair and sat down beside her.

"Cat got your tongue?" he asked, a satisfied smirk on his face.

"Actually, no," she said, with more bravado than she felt. "I'm just wondering how long it's going to take for you to figure out who I am."

Wanting to smack the smirk off his face, she lowered her hands into her lap and clasped them tightly together.

"I don't think I've ever seen you before pretty woman," he said smugly. Leaning nearer as he spoke, Meredith felt nauseous as his sour beer breath permeated her nose. She stiffened. "I'm sure I would have remembered you," he went on. "I'm Taylor Boone and you are?"

Regaining her composure, Meredith paused before speaking. Looking Taylor directly in the eye she said, "I've been away a long time so you may not recognize me. However, I do remember you…vividly."

Taylor frowned, clearly puzzled.

"I'm Meredith Banning."

Taylor's eyes widened with surprise. He jumped out of his chair, toppling it over. "You can't be," he said, rubbing his forehead with one hand while trying to right the chair with the other and hang onto his beer at the same time. "Why, Meredith Banning is…"

"What Taylor? A tub of lard? Bubble butt? Fatty-fatty two-by-four? Those were just a few of the names you chose to call me," she snapped. "The others escape me at the moment."

Old anxieties reared their ugly heads and a sick feeling settled in the pit of her stomach. One small encounter with Taylor Boone and she was an angry mess, transported back to a time in her life that she had struggled to forget.

Not skipping a beat and seemingly amused by her revelation, Taylor said, "Well, all I have to say is you've come a long way baby." Waving his arms, he hollered across the room. "Hey everyone, look who's back. It's Meredith Banning!"

Every head turned in her direction, mouths gaping in disbelief.

The old Meredith wanted to crawl under the table, but the new and improved Meredith wanted to jump up and shout, "How do you like me now?" Instead, she remained riveted to her chair.

Taylor squeezed Meredith's shoulder. She cringed from his touch. "Lighten up, doll. You're tighter than a tick. Catch you later."

She heard him laugh while she watched him swagger back to his friends, taking another pull off his beer. God how she hated him still. Reeling from repressed anger, she didn't see the woman coming to her table.

"Meredith?"

Jumpy as spit on a skillet, she turned her head toward the intruder. "What?" she spat."

"Meredith, it's me, Carrie…Carrie Owens. I heard you were back. You sure have changed. You look wonderful," she gushed. "You'll have to tell me your secret."

Carrie Owens, high school girlfriend of Taylor, had been another tormentor of Meredith's. The once tiny, blond cheerleader surrounded by hangers-on wanting to be just like her, now stood before her; a short, plump, frizzy-haired Carrie with no hangers-on at all. Carrie grabbed a chair, scraping it along the floor and positioned it next to Meredith.

"Mind if I sit down?" she asked, dropping heavily into the chair. "Some of the girls told me you were here. They pointed you out and I couldn't believe it was you."

Anger flared in Meredith's eyes. "Taylor just announced to the whole damn gym I was here so I'm surprised you didn't hear him."

"I was in the ladies room," she said, almost sadly, as if she had missed all the fun. "You've never been to a reunion before so this is quite a surprise."

"Velvet passed away and I have some business to attend to. Otherwise I wouldn't be here." Velvet, Meredith's mother, had refused to let her daughter call her mom because it made her feel old. "Since it was reunion time and I was in the area, I decided to attend. I see not much has changed."

"We heard about your mother. So very sorry. Will you be staying a while or do you plan to go back to…where was it? Florida or something like that?"

Ignoring her question, Meredith went on. "I'm not sure what I'm going to do yet. I have some loose ends to tie up, and then I'm going to take a much-needed vacation before I make any decisions. I'm sure you'll be seeing me around."

5

"Well, maybe we can get together for lunch one of these days."

It'll be a cold day in hell.

"I'd better be getting back to Taylor. We got married you know. Had to. Been married going on eighteen years now. We have three boys, one graduating this year. There's some food over there on the tables if you're hungry."

"Thanks, but I think I'll pass."

"I'll tell the other girls you're here. I'm sure they'll be over to say hey." Carrie stood up and gave Meredith a little wave good-bye. "See ya," she said.

The DJ spun *Always on my Mind* and more couples moved out onto the dance floor. A slow song had always been the perfect excuse for bumping, grinding and getting as close as one could get with clothes still on.

Meredith sat alone, watching, just as she had done all those years ago; praying for someone to ask her to dance, praying that they wouldn't. Deciding she'd had enough for one evening, she stood and turned to leave.

"Hold on little lady." A man's large hand grasped her arm.

Meredith's heart skipped a beat and her mouth went dry. A tingle of anxiety prickled the back of her neck. Slowly she turned at the sound of a voice her heart knew well. She looked into the dark brown eyes of her one and only friend in Stony Creek.

Releasing her arm, Dakota Morgan, brows drawn together in a scowl asked, "Are you going to run away like you did twenty years ago or stay and dance with me?" He held out a hand to her and silently she took it.

6

CHAPTER TWO

DAKOTA LED MEREDITH TO the dance floor, his long jet-black hair pulled into a neat ponytail. He was handsome, in a rough sort of way, with high cheekbones, straight nose, and deep set brown eyes. Proud of his Black Foot and Caucasian heritage, he resembled the Native American culture more than his mother's side of the family, although his stature was tall, nearly six feet. A muscle jerked in his cheek as he peered down at her, willing her to look back at him.

Still holding his hand, Meredith sucked in her breath and stared into his chocolate eyes. "You sure got big," she said, a smile breaking across her face. *Brilliant, Meredith, just brilliant!* "What I meant to say was you sure are tall. It's really good to see you, Dakota."

Dakota said nothing but continued to look intently at Meredith. Gently he put his right hand on her waist and took her right hand in his. She put her left hand on his shoulder, feeling his tightly defined muscles beneath her fingers. Drawing her close he began to move them easily to the music, as if they'd danced together forever.

Meredith could feel calluses on his hand and smell his musky manly scent. As they slowly swayed to the music, she thought she could feel something else, too. Wow! Heart be still! She let her thoughts wander trying to erase the image from her mind. Laying her head on his chest, she felt his rapid heartbeat beneath his shirt. When the music ended, Dakota asked, although it was more a command than a question, "Let's get out of here for a while." She nodded.

Walking off the dance floor, Meredith heard murmurs from the men and something about, "There she goes with that half-breed again." Certain that Dakota heard she glanced at him.

"Pay them no mind. Sticks and stones, Meredith, sticks and stones." Eyes straight ahead, he placed his hand on her elbow and led her out through the gymnasium doors.

"Those guys still haven't grown up," she said disgustedly. "They're just as bad as they were in high school and now they call themselves men. I don't think so."

The evening air was warm. Holding her hand, Dakota led her across the parking lot to a nearby bench beneath the base of an old, gnarly cottonwood tree. "Sit, *please*," he said.

DAKOTA MORGAN HAD BEEN MEREDITH'S only friend when she was growing up. His parents, Anna and Yuma Morgan, worked for her grandparents as caretakers of their ranch.

Anna Jenkins, daughter of a local drifter who left her to fend for herself much of the time, fell in love with Yuma Morgan, a full blood Blackfoot Indian. They met one summer while working on the same ranch. After a short and secret courtship, they eloped to a neighboring state when they were barely seventeen years old. Returning to Stony Creek, Yuma and Anna found employment nearly impossible because of their interracial marriage. Charlie Parker, Meredith's grandfather, offered them jobs. It was on his hundred-acre ranch that the two youngsters met and worked together that summer. He knew them to be hard working and responsible, and he needed the help.

8

Anna's job consisted of taking charge of the household and Yuma was Charlie's right-hand-man tending to the land and the livestock. They were loyal employees and paid a decent wage for their efforts. Over the years, as the ranch became more prosperous and more hands were hired, Charlie promoted Yuma to foreman.

Dakota was born three years later in the small caretaker's bungalow, three months before Charlie and Doris's daughter, Velvet, gave birth to Meredith.

Velvet never enjoyed being a mother and found it difficult taking care of a newborn. She couldn't tolerate her crying baby, and hated that she had lost her girlish figure. Anna not only tended to Dakota, but also took over the job of wet-nursing Meredith when Velvet refused to breastfeed. The two babies grew up happy and healthy under the nurturing care of Anna. Playmates as little children, they became best friends as they grew older.

THE TWO CHILDREN STARTED SCHOOL when they were six years old and from day one, it was hell for the both of them. Dakota's peers tormented him because he was half-Indian. His reddish-colored skin, high cheekbones beneath his dark brown eyes, and long black hair set him aside from the other boys with their white skin, lighter hair and shorter stature.

On Dakota's first day of school, Yuma sat him down for a heart-to-heart talk. He was such a little boy, but Yuma knew what could lay in store for his child.

"My son. I will tell you this one time only and you must remember. You are different from the other boys you will meet in school and some of them will not be nice to you."

"Why, Father?"

"Because they don't know any better, Dakota. You must not fight with the other boys, even if they call you names. You

9

must turn the other cheek and stay out of trouble so you can go to school." Yuma's gut contracted in a hard, painful knot because of the heavy burden he was laying on his only son. He hugged him tightly, stood, and walked out of the room.

Dakota did his best to stay out of trouble like his father told him to, but there were times when he couldn't help himself.

Meredith, bullied and persecuted because she was overweight, was no match for her tormenters. She was frightened and intimidated by them and they used it to their advantage.

Her brown hair was naturally curly and unruly. No matter how vigorously Velvet tried to tame her daughter's hair, it had a mind of its own. Not only overweight with crazy brown hair, she also wore ugly brown-rimmed glasses. "Fatty, fatty, four-eyes," they would taunt her.

Crying, she would run to Dakota and grab onto his shirt. "Did you hear what they called me?"

Dakota couldn't stand to see Meredith cry. He would beat up the boys who called her names and in the process would get into trouble, occasionally suspended for fighting. By the time he arrived home from school, Yuma would be waiting for him to mete out his own punishment. There were many trips to the woodshed because of Dakota's chivalry.

Dakota was Meredith's protector all the years they were growing up. When he was sixteen, he realized that he was in love with her. He would have walked over hot coals for her; that is, until the end of their senior year. It was graduation time and the prom was a few days away. He asked Meredith to go with him months ago and she'd happily agreed.

Three days before the prom, Meredith was at her locker putting her books away when Taylor Boone came up to her. "Hey, Meredith, ah, sorry it's so late, but I wanted to know if you would go to the senior prom with me on Friday."

10

Meredith's jaw dropped open. Her heart felt like it was bursting out of her chest. Without thinking, she sputtered, "I'd love to go with you."

"Good, I thought you would," he said. Grinning, he walked towards his friends. They laughed loudly and slapped each other on the back. Taylor hollered over to Meredith. "Oh, I'll pick you up at seven o'clock," and they burst into laughter again.

She stood there blushing and nodded. Meredith was so excited she could hardly stand it. She couldn't believe that hunky Taylor Boone had asked her to the prom. She never stopped to wonder why he wasn't taking Carrie Owens.

Later that day, she and Dakota got off the school bus. Walking down the dirt road to the ranch, she broke the news to him. "I…ah, I hope you won't be too upset with me, but Taylor Boone asked me to the prom and I told him I'd go."

"You did *what*?" he asked, nostrils flaring. "How could you possibly agree to go anywhere with him after the way he's treated you all these years?"

"I know. You're right. But it's something I really want to do so I'm going to do it."

Dakota tried to hide the hurt he was feeling as he clenched and unclenched his fists. For a minute, he thought he might even cry so he turned his head away from her. "What about *me*, Meredith? You told me you'd go to the prom with *me*."

"I know I did. I'm sorry, Dakota. Can you even imagine what it's like to finally be accepted by people that have always looked down on us?"

"No, I guess I can't imagine it since it's never happened to me."

"We'll still be friends, right?" she asked, yanking on his shirtsleeve.

Stony Creek Diner

Dakota said nothing and broke off into a sprint leaving Meredith behind in the dust. Cupping her hands around her mouth, she called after him, "Da-ko-ta." He never turned around, just kept running as if he had a bear on his tail.

CHAPTER THREE

MEREDITH COULDN'T WAIT TO tell her parents about her date. Entering the house she slammed the door behind her and hollered, "Velvet, Daddy, I'm home. I have something wonderful to tell you."

"This had better be good," Velvet said, coming down from upstairs. "I was taking a nap until you made such a ruckus."

Dallas came into the room from the kitchen where he had been preparing the evening meal. "What's up little girl?" he asked.

"Humph, little. Right," Velvet said with sarcasm.

"That's enough," Dallas challenged, anger flaring in his eyes.

"Tell us what the big news is, honey," Dallas urged.

"Taylor Boone asked me to the senior prom!"

"Well, isn't that wonderful. When is the prom?" Dallas asked.

"Friday night. I know it's soon, but he wasn't sure he was going to go until today."

Velvet was elated that *finally* a popular boy asked her daughter on a date, never mind that he might be from the wrong side of the tracks. At least he wasn't a half-breed. As much as she cared for the Morgan's, she did not want her daughter dating anyone except a white boy.

"We'll go to Bozeman tomorrow and get you a dress," she said. "Be up early because I don't want to be gone all day."

"Okay, I will." Meredith ran up the stairs to her bedroom, happier than she had ever been.

THE NEXT MORNING, MEREDITH AND VELVET left the ranch for the sixty-mile drive to Bozeman. Meredith was excited to be spending a day with her mother; a very rare occasion.

On the grassy hillsides near the highway, antelope were playing and further on up the hill a herd of bison were quietly grazing. Several babies bounded up and down kicking their feet high as if playing kickball.

A split second later Velvet let out an expletive and slammed on the brakes, nearly going into a skid, as a gopher ran in front of her. Eyes wide he ran to the right, then to the left, and then under the wheels of the car. They felt a thud. "Damn."

The rest of the drive was uneventful. Finding a parking spot at the mall was not an easy feat. They circled three or four times before a spot became available. Velvet nearly caused an accident trying to maneuver into a spot so another person couldn't get it.

Shopping for three hours with no luck, they went from one store to another. "It's hard to believe we can't find one single dress that fits your body and looks decent!" Disgusted, Velvet moved through the mall as if she was running a 5K.

"I'm sorry, Velvet," Meredith said softly, hurrying behind her mother to keep up. The day was turning out to be a disaster instead of the wonderful mother-daughter adventure that Meredith had envisioned.

Just about the time her mother was ready to come unglued, and Meredith was about to burst into tears, they spied a Fashion Barn. Velvet would sooner slit her own wrists than go into a plus size store, but at this point, she was desperate. She grabbed Meredith by the arm and pushed her inside.

"I suppose we better start over here." Velvet let out a loud sigh, ushering Meredith towards the women's section.

"You better hope we can find something soon or you won't be going to the prom at all," she threatened, grabbing one dress after another off the rack and thrusting them into Meredith's arms. "Take these into the dressing room. I'll wait outside. If you find one that fits, come out and model it for me." Velvet paced back and forth. *I should have made Anna bring her shopping instead of me. This has turned into a monumental fiasco.*

Meredith went into the changing room, hating the whole ordeal that buying a dress had become and hoping one would fit. After trying on several items, they found a lovely deep burgundy dress that was the perfect color and size for Meredith. She felt like a princess in her first grown-up dress and for the first time in her life, she felt beautiful. They made one last stop on the way home for some black short-heeled pumps.

Arriving home, Velvet poured a shot of her father's dandelion wine, took to her bed, exhausted and frazzled. *Never again.*

Meredith went searching for Dakota, but he was keeping a low profile and she couldn't locate him. The day with her mother had been brutal and she needed a shoulder to cry on.

Friday rolled around and Meredith felt a rush of happiness. In a few short hours, she would be going on her first date and to her first dance with the boy of her dreams. She hadn't talked to Taylor since he asked her out, but he had seen her in the hallway and waved. That was enough for her, especially since Dakota was making himself scarce. He no longer rode the school bus, and they'd had no contact since she told him she was going to the prom with Taylor.

Velvet asked Anna for help getting Meredith ready for the prom, but Anna, never one to say no, said no. As much as she loved Meredith, she was fiercely protective of her son's feelings. For once, she was choosing sides.

At seven o'clock Meredith came down the stairs wearing her new dress and shoes. Her hair, fluffed up softly, looked very becoming. She wore a scant bit of makeup; soft green eye shadow, a little blush and lipstick. She wore contacts instead of her glasses.

"You look beautiful, honey," Dallas said, waiting at the bottom of the stairs for her. He snapped several pictures of the moment. She smiled at him and hugged him around the neck. Her father always made her feel special and she knew how much he loved her. Velvet stayed in her room complaining of a headache and said she'd be down later.

"I wish Gramps and Gram were here to see me," she said wistfully. They were in Colorado buying livestock.

"I'll get these pictures developed tomorrow," Dallas promised. You'll be able to show them how beautiful you looked in your prom dress when they get home."

At seven-thirty Meredith was still waiting for Taylor to arrive, looking out the window every few minutes when she thought she heard a car coming down the drive. By eight-thirty, tears streaming down her face, she knew that Taylor wasn't coming.

She couldn't stand the look of pity, or was that shame, on her parents' faces, especially Velvet's, so she dashed out of the house. Kicking off her shoes, she hurried across the field until she came to the little brook that ran through the property. Falling to the ground, she covered her face. Deep shaking sobs wracked her body.

Minutes later, she felt a warm hand on her shoulder. "Meredith, come here." She turned and looked at Dakota. Anna told him what happened. He held his arms out to her and she let him envelop her into the safety that she had always felt with him.

"I was such a fool. I'm so sorry, Dakota."

"Hush. It's okay. Let's get you home now." He helped her up and led her back across the field. "I'll see you tomorrow, okay?"

"Okay."

Twenty minutes later Taylor Boone was lying on his back in the school parking lot where he had just taken a beating by Dakota Morgan who was now sitting in jail.

CHAPTER FOUR

SITTING ON THE WOODEN BENCH, Meredith glanced at Dakota. She nervously twisted the ring on her right index finger round and round while she spoke. "I'm so sorry I left town while you were sitting in jail because of me."

"I wasn't in jail because of you. I was in jail because of me. I didn't have to beat the tar out of Taylor, but it sure felt good when I did. He deserved it."

"I didn't forgive myself for a long time," she said sadly, shaking her head. "I jeopardized the only friendship I ever had and for what? Nothing. Were you in jail very long?"

Dakota shook his head. "No, only for a few days. Taylor didn't press charges although I was sure he would. I don't know why he had a change of heart, but I never questioned it. Where did you go? No one would tell me."

"My grandfather was the only one who knew where I was for quite a while. He wouldn't even tell Velvet or my dad where I'd gone. He just told them I was safe and for them not to worry."

Her chin quivered. Dakota was afraid she was going to cry and he couldn't stand that. It took her a few minutes before she got her emotions under control. "Gramps finally gave dad my phone number and we stayed in contact until he disappeared. Velvet never wrote or called. It was years before I spoke to her again. She never wanted kids and told me so."

18

"I'm sorry about your dad going missing and now the death of Velvet. It's a lot to handle. I'm so lucky to have my parents. They love you, too, you know."

Meredith scooted over so Dakota could sit next to her. "I know they do and I'm grateful. Gramps took care of me financially until I was able to support myself. I don't know what I would have done without him."

"So where *did* you go? Why didn't you write? I was half-crazy wondering where you were. Didn't you know I loved you and would have taken care of you?"

Meredith felt a pang of regret, but didn't answer his question. "Once I made the decision to leave Stony Creek I wanted to get as far away as possible, so I chose Maine.

"Maine? Why on earth would you pick Maine?"

"Velvet used to give me her old magazines when she was done with them. They were full of advertisements for travel brochures and I would send for them. I was so excited when they showed up in the mailbox."

She took a breath and closed her eyes, recalling how she felt back then. "I would run up to my bedroom and spend hours going through every page of them. They became a means of escape for me. For some reason I always felt an affinity to New England." She let out a breath before continuing "I'd never been farther east than Billings, but I could dream. I think I subconsciously laid out a plan long before I left."

"Did you always intend to leave? It took me a long time before I could admit that you were never coming back. Tell me more about Maine."

"I'd never seen the ocean, walked in the sand or marveled at the brilliant New England foliage. I wanted to experience it all and Maine seemed to fit all my wants. Once there, I fell in love with the beaches and small fishing towns, and I made some wonderful friends." She stopped to draw a breath. "Oh, listen to me, going on about myself all this time. Sorry I've been rambling on so much."

Dakota hunched forward, elbows on knees, chin resting on his hands before speaking. "Did you find what it was you were running from?"

"I think I did," she said. "I was running away from me. I hated the way I looked, hated the way others looked at me, hated the taunts and sneers, but most of all I hated my mother for never sticking up for me."

"I had no idea you were feeling so terrible. You never mentioned it. I guess men are just dopes." He took off his hat, turned it around a few times, and put it back on his head. "Well pretty lady, you sure are looking fine these days, although to me you were always beautiful."

Meredith reached for his hand and covered it with hers. There was an awkward silence before she spoke. "I'm sorry if I hurt you. I knew that you loved me as I did you, but honestly, I never knew that you were *in* love with me."

"Would you have stayed if you'd known?"

She shrugged her shoulders. "I don't know. At the time I just knew I had to get away."

"How long did you stay in Maine? Your Gramps eventually told me that you moved to Florida. I wouldn't stop badgering him so I think he told me just to shut me up. He never did give me your address though."

"I only stayed in Maine a year. I lived in a little town on the coast, joined a weight loss program, and started taking care of myself. I found a job in a seafood restaurant as a short-order cook. Who would have thought that, huh?" she said, smiling at him. "It was a huge challenge, too, especially since I discovered I love seafood and was trying to lose weight at the same time."

Looking somewhat confused, Dakota pressed her to tell him more. He knew nothing about losing weight and had never eaten seafood. In fact, he was sure he never would. He was content to listen to Meredith for as long as she wanted to talk.

"Go on," he urged. "I've waited twenty years to hear this story."

"What exactly do you want to know? I've been gone a long time, Dakota."

"Tell me everything." He sat back, crossing his ankle over his knee.

"I worked really hard at losing weight. I exercised by running on the beach and taking long walks every day. I weighed every morsel of food that I put in my mouth and it finally started to pay off. As the weight came off, I began to like myself more. I gained self-confidence, too, something I'd never had. Walking down the street no one looked at me twice, or if they did, it was in an admiring way. The first time a man whistled at me I almost fell over dead," she chuckled.

Dakota gave her a strained smile, feeling a little jealous. He wanted to be the one that whistled at Meredith.

"I also found a good counselor who helped me get rid of many old issues that were keeping me stuck in a bad place. Once I was where I wanted to be mentally and physically, I called Gramps. I told him I had been thinking about attending a culinary school in Florida to become a chef. I asked if he would pay my tuition and he gladly agreed. I enjoyed cooking and was good at it. My plan was to become a diet chef, planning healthy meals and menus for people trying to lose weight."

"So you went ahead with your plans, then?"

"I was a little concerned that I would gain the weight back, but that was a risk I was willing to take. I felt I had a handle on it and knew what were good and bad foods. I had my struggles and temptations though, but I liked where I was, what I looked like, and with Gramps's help I went for it."

"So you're actually a chef now?"

21

"I have been, for eighteen years. In fact, I'm an executive chef."

"What is it that you do?" He didn't know the first thing about being a chef either.

"I manage a kitchen in a wonderful establishment and manage a team of 10 kitchen workers. I plan the daily menu and order the food. I also train new employees, assign tasks, and make sure the kitchen runs smoothly. We have a great crew who all work well together."

"I'm impressed," Dakota said smiling. "What are your plans now?"

"I don't know yet. I'm taking some time off to decide, but I *will* be around for a while. We've talked a lot about me, so what about you? Gramps refused to tell me about you, too. He said when I was ready I could ask you myself. Are you married?" She didn't know why, but she hoped not.

Just as Dakota was about to answer, the gym doors burst open.

CHAPTER FIVE

TAYLOR STAGGERED DRUNKENLY out into the parking lot accompanied by his two pals, Jackson Weaver and Ernie Loomis. Loud, boisterous and obnoxious he was looking for trouble and Dakota was his target.

"Are you going to keep the pretty little miss to yourself, Morgan?" Taylor shouted.

Meredith looked at them contemptuously and started to get up. Dakota abruptly stood, put his hand on her shoulder and pushed her back down onto the bench. "Stay there," he commanded.

His eyes narrowed and his face turned hard, but he said nothing. *If I have to beat him, I will,* but he wasn't looking forward to going to jail again. Three against one wouldn't be a fair fight but Dakota knew he could handle himself.

"It's time me and the boys got a little piece of *that*," Taylor smirked, jerking his head toward Meredith. He elbowed Ernie in the ribs. "C'mon," he ordered, teetering across the lot to where she was sitting. Ernie and Jackson followed, but at a safe distance. Dakota took a step forward.

The doors to the gym opened and Carrie stepped outside. She ran over to her husband and grabbed him by the arm. "You're drunk, Taylor. Don't cause no one any trouble. Come back inside with me," she urged.

Taylor spun around. "Get off me, bitch," he yelled, throwing her to the ground. She cried out as she hit the dirt.

Without thinking, Meredith flew off the bench. In her quest to help Carrie, she slammed against Taylor with her elbow and heard a loud 'oomph' as she connected with his gut.

Dakota scooped Carrie off the ground and stood her on her feet. Meredith helped brush the dirt from her hair and dress. "Are you all right?" she asked. Carrie nodded and wiped the tears from her face.

Losing his balance from the unexpected blow to his mid-section, Taylor's boots slipped on the sharp gravel sending him headlong onto the ground. "My nose," he cried, blood spurting all over. "My fucking nose is broken!" Reaching behind him, he pulled a handkerchief from his back pocket and held it against his bleeding snout.

For one crazy moment, all was quiet. Ernie and Jackson stood wide-eyed, mouths ajar. They couldn't believe what they had just witnessed. Mousy Meredith Banning had dropped Taylor Boone like a bag of hot coals.

Rushing over to help him, Taylor rewarded them with the finger. "Leave me the hell alone." He struggled to sit and eventually stood. On his feet, he hollered at Carrie. "Girl, you get the truck and take me the hell home."

With a protective arm around Carrie's shoulder, Meredith looked at the once popular girl, now an abused wife. "Can I drive you somewhere?" She still didn't like Carrie, but she would not stand idly by and watch Taylor misuse her.

"No, but thanks anyway. I've got my boys at home to tend to. I'll be okay. This wasn't too bad. I've dealt with worse."

"Are you sure? I don't mind giving you a ride."

"I'm sure," she said, eyes filling up with tears again.

"Carrie!" Taylor yelled, wincing from the pain of his broken nose. He doubled his fists and made a threatening gesture, but didn't move toward her. "Didn't you hear me, woman? I told you to go get the truck."

She pulled away from the safety of Meredith's arm and ran inside the gym to retrieve their belongings. Seeing Carrie's distress, her girlfriends hurried over to her to see if they could help.

"How much longer are you going to put up with this, Carrie?" Julia Loomis asked her.

"Take the boys and leave," Sandra Weaver told her.

"And where would you expect me to go?" she cried. "How would I support me and the boys? I've never worked a day in my life." Rigid with fear she cried, "I can't leave even if I want to. Taylor would track me down and kill me if I took those boys away." Looking at her friends she said, "He would, too, and you both know it." She grabbed her sweater and purse and started towards the gym door.

"Carrie, wait," Julia called, running after her. "You forgot Taylor's jacket." She held it out to her.

Outside, Taylor glared at Meredith and Dakota. "This ain't over," he yelled, shaking his fist at them. "I'm not done with either of you yet. You just wait and see!"

DRIVING DOWN THE DIRT ROAD to their mobile home, Carrie looked over at Taylor. As soon as he was in the truck, he had fallen asleep and was snoring loudly. She prayed he wouldn't wake up until morning. If not, she knew what was coming.

CARRIE OWENS, PETITE, BLOND-HAIRED and blue eyed was the most sought-after girl in high school, until she fell in love with Taylor Boone her sophomore year. From the day they met, they were inseparable; that is, except for a six-month break-up when Taylor hit her during a jealous rage. Carrie refused to speak to him for three months after the incident. Her father threatened to kill him for hurting his baby girl.

Taylor pursued Carrie relentlessly, begging her to forgive him. "Carrie, honey, please forgive me," he pleaded, tears streaming down his face. "I'm so sorry. I was so afraid of losing you when I saw you talking to Howard that I just lost it. I never would have hit you if *you* hadn't made me so jealous."

He professed over and again how much he loved her; how he couldn't live without her, and vowed never to put his hands on her again. Eventually Carrie broke down and forgave him. She believed Taylor's every word and he kept his promise…for a while.

Carrie's parents, Larry and Linda Owens, were completely against their daughter dating Taylor. They hadn't approved of her dating him before he hit Carrie, but let her go out with him hoping that she would see he was not the boy she thought he was. After he hit her, they were beside themselves.

"Carrie, Taylor *will* hit you again the next time you do something that makes him jealous or mad," Linda reasoned.

"No he won't," she cried. "He promised me and I believe him."

"We don't want you seeing him anymore. If you don't obey us, young lady," Larry threatened, "then we'll send you to Aunt Lucy's in Oklahoma and you can go to school there."

Carrie didn't budge. She was in love and nothing was going to stop her from being with Taylor. She sneaked out of the house several times and eventually her father caught her.

After a horrible scene with accusations, threats and yelling, her parents gave in. Their biggest fear was that Carrie would get pregnant on purpose to be with Taylor if they kept her from seeing him. Sending her away was not an option; they couldn't bear being apart from their only child.

THE NEXT TWO YEARS SPED BY without incident. Larry and Linda admitted to each other that perhaps they had been wrong about Taylor. Carrie seemed happy with him, was doing well in school, and all seemed right in their world.

Just before graduation, their biggest fear became a reality. Carrie announced that she was pregnant. Larry and Linda were going to be grandparents.

A few weeks after graduation, Carrie and Taylor wed in the little Methodist chapel on Willow Hill. The Reverend Storm Anderson officiated. Reverend Anderson, only a few years older than Carrie and Taylor, was considered Stony Creek's most eligible bachelor.

Seven months later, Gage Jacob Boone burst into the world screaming and kicking, followed by Dustin (Dusty) Taylor Boone twelve months after his brother. Eight years later, their surprise baby, Daniel Larry Boone, made his arrival.

Shortly after Dusty was born, Taylor was injured in an accident. After an evening of drinking beer with his friends, they climbed a fence corralling a herd of longhorn cattle. Wanting to prove his prowess, Taylor decided to go bull riding.

Shining his flashlight throughout the pasture, he spotted the bull. His friends egged him on, hooting and hollering, "Go git him, Taylor. Ride that big boy."

They watched as Taylor ran over to the bull, grabbed one of his horns and tried to swing onto his back. The bull threw him into the air and he landed on the ground with a terrible thud, knocking the wind out of him. Before he could move out of the way, the bull snorted and charged Taylor, goring him in the leg, damaging muscle and breaking his femur.

His scream paralyzed his friends, and it was seconds before they could move to help him. Two of them ran into the pasture, hollering at the bull and waving their hats to get his attention off Taylor. The other two ran to Taylor, grabbed him under the arms and pulled him to safety.

He spent the next month in the hospital, a blessed relief for Carrie. After his wounds healed, Taylor walked with a nasty limp, making him feel less than a man and giving him an excuse to drink more heavily.

Unable to find work after his injury, except for part-time jobs here and there, Taylor's temper flared at the slightest provocation. His wife was usually the recipient of his rage. On occasion, he went after the boys. Carrie would step in to protect them, paying for it dearly after she shooed them off to their room.

The boys were the glue that kept Carrie stuck in what had become a total hell, married to an abusive alcoholic. Her sons were the most important people in her life. Promising herself that she would suffer whatever consequences came her way, she vowed to keep her family intact.

Trips to town were embarrassing for Carrie. As hard as she tried, she couldn't cover up the black and blue marks on her arms or more than once the black eyes. All of Stony Creek knew of the abuse.

Her father once again threatened to kill Taylor or at the very least have him killed, but Carrie pleaded with him to stay out of it. She would manage on her own.

TURNING INTO THEIR DRIVEWAY, Taylor shifted in his seat. He let out a loud belch, then a fart, but didn't wake up. Turning off the ignition, she waited before opening her door. Taylor stirred again. Carrie held her breath.

CHAPTER SIX

"THIS WAS CERTAINLY an interesting evening," Meredith said as she and Dakota walked arm in arm through the parking lot back to her car.

"Whenever drinking is involved, you can count on Taylor Boone showing up and causing problems. This wasn't the first time and it won't be the last."

Meredith directed Dakota toward a sleek, shiny Mercedes. He looked at her, eyebrows raised. Grinning, she said, "I know it's a bit much. I'm not usually this extravagant, but I bought her on a whim and I've never been sorry." Motioning towards her car, "I'd like to introduce you to *Mercedes*."

"You named your car? Figures," Dakota grumbled. "Your grandfather names everything, too. Where are you staying anyway?"

"Gramps wanted me to stay with him, but I thought it would be best to stay at Velvet's. There's a mountain of memories in that house, not all good, and I've got lots of cleaning out to do."

"If you weren't driving this flamboyant piece of metal, I would offer you a ride."

"You can follow me home if you'd like," she said with a twinkle in her eye. Smiling at him and feeling a nervous tingle in her tummy she said, "I make a mean cup of coffee."

Sweat broke out across Dakota's upper lip and he rotated the brim of his hat while deciding whether to take her up on her offer. He loved her, but didn't want to risk opening old wounds that were still raw after all these years. He checked his watch. "Thanks, but it's late and I've got a big day ahead of me tomorrow. I think I'll call it a night. Maybe some other time?"

"Are you sure? It's only coffee and small talk. I really want us to be friends again."

"I'm sure. I'll give you a call in a few days or stop by if you're still around."

Meredith nodded, feeling rejected and somewhat confused by Dakota's actions. She got behind the wheel of *Mercedes*, started her up, and waved good-bye. Slamming her foot on the accelerator, she spun gravel all the way out of the parking lot.

"*Damn fool woman. She's going to get herself killed driving like that,*" Dakota mused, admiring the feisty spirit that she now showed. He was going to enjoy getting to know the new Meredith.

THE FOLLOWING MORNING, Meredith woke to the sun bursting in through her bedroom window. She rolled onto her back and lay there listening to the sounds she had long forgotten.

Hearing the deep, rolling trumpet of the sand hill cranes in the pasture and the rich fluty whistle of the meadowlark, a longing to come home overcame her. A hawk screeched as he hunted for mice, and off in the distance she heard a coyote howl.

Slowly she climbed out of bed and reached for her plush, fuzzy robe lying on the cedar chest. Grabbing a pair of socks from her suitcase she put them on her feet, slippers forgotten when she packed. Montana mornings in early June were a bit cool. Folding her arms across her chest to help ward off the chill, she walked over to the window and peered out.

Gazing at the vista before her, she caught her breath. Standing majestic and snow-covered were her beloved Tobacco Root mountains. They were miles away, but on a clear day such as this, they looked close enough to touch.

Moving away from the window, she glanced around her room. In the twenty years she'd been gone, nothing had changed. Posters of Patrick Swayze, Tom Cruise, and Keanu Reeves, who resembled Dakota, still adorned her walls. Brochures from Maine to California were stacked in her bookcase. Teddy bears and blond-haired Barbie dolls lounged in a blue easy chair in the corner

Walking across the room, she opened the door to her closet. Her eyes widened, she gasped and her hand went to her mouth. Her clothes, dusty and faded, were hanging exactly where she had left them. She reached in and removed a blouse.

Holding the large floral fabric in front of her, tears filled her eyes remembering how her life had been as a fat girl. Rubbing her forehead, she frowned. Why had her mother left them hanging here all these years? Was this Velvet's way of punishing her from the grave; reminding Meredith that she was the daughter her mother would forever be ashamed of?

She scurried away from the closet, dropping the blouse on the floor, and ran out of the room. Hurt and angry at Velvet, she hurried down the steps, two at a time, and rushed into the kitchen. Stomping over to the counter, she snapped the "on" button on the coffee pot.

Waiting for the coffee to brew, and in an act of defiance, she threw a bag of popcorn into the microwave and shoved a Snicker's bar, which had been hiding in her purse, into her mouth. If she wanted popcorn and candy for breakfast, by God she would have it. "Take that, *MOTHER*," she hissed!

The phone rang. Agitated, Meredith picked it up and yelled into the receiver. "What!"

"Meredith? What's wrong, honey? It's Gramps."

"I'm sorry, Gramps. It's been kind of a tough morning being in this house again."

"You can still come over and stay with me."

"I really do need to stay here," she said. "There are things that I have to do. I hope you understand."

"I understand, honey. I'm going into town in a while. Would you like to come with me? There's something I'd like to show you."

Meredith would have preferred staying put, but she didn't want to disappoint her grandfather. "Sure, what time will you pick me up or better yet, would you like a ride in the Mercedes?"

"I think I'll pass on that. I saw Dakota this morning and he told me you left the school parking lot on two wheels last night." She heard him chuckle.

"I did no such thing and he knows it."

"I'll pick you up around eleven o'clock, if that's good for you."

"I'll be ready. Love you, Gramps."

"Love you, too, little girl."

Hanging up, Meredith reached for the bag of popcorn and discarded it. Now that her emotional crisis was over, the already devoured Snicker's bar would energize her for several hours. She poured herself a cup of coffee and glanced at the clock. It was only eight and she had three hours before her grandfather would pick her up.

She seated herself at the table in front of the bay window and once again marveled at the sight of the Tobacco Roots. Off to her right were the Cottonwoods. Just beyond the trees was the small brook where Dakota found her many years ago after her humiliation on prom night. That wound still felt raw and Meredith doubted it would ever go away.

Hearing a knock at the front door she got up to answer it. "Hey," she said to Dakota who was standing on the porch, hat in his hands. Not seeing a car or truck, she noticed his Buckskin horse tethered to a makeshift hitching post at the side of the driveway. The Buckskin was happily nibbling away on the green grass.

"Thought I'd come by to make sure you got home in one piece last night."

"You've obviously been by my grandfather's, and now he won't ride with me. Thanks a lot."

His eyes crinkled when he smiled at her and it looked to Meredith like he was trying to stifle a laugh. "You're not laughing at me are you?" she cautioned, eyes narrowing to tiny slits.

"Hell, no," Dakota said, bursting out laughing. Meredith slammed the door in his face. Laughing louder he knocked again and again until she opened the door.

As much as she tried not to, Meredith eked out a tiny grin. "Do you want some coffee?" she asked, trying to act disgusted, but not doing a good job of it.

Dakota hurried into the house before she had a chance to change her mind. Smirking, he took a seat.

"Knock it off or you'll find yourself on the other side of the door again." She slapped a mug of coffee on the table in front of him, spilling some of its contents. Grabbing a paper towel she wiped the spill away while Dakota sat there grinning like an idiot.

Sitting down next to him, Meredith asked, "Do you know what my grandfather wants to show me?"

"Yup," he responded, taking a sip of the scalding liquid.

"Well, are you going to tell me?"

"Nope," he said, eyeing Meredith up and down. Realizing that she was wearing only her fuzzy robe and little else, she pulled her robe tighter around her and gave Dakota the evil eye.

"You'd better get dressed," he said, ogling her.

"You'd better drink your coffee and get out of here," she retorted, thinking that Dakota was hot, hot, hot; more handsome as he had gotten older, if that was possible.

In his denim shirt with leather vest and faded blue jeans, he smirked at her as if he knew exactly what she was thinking. Abruptly he stood, pulled her to him by her shoulders, and ever so lightly brushed his lips against hers. Just as abruptly, he let her go and walked out of the house.

Shaken to her very core, she tugged her robe even closer. What was that all about? She watched from the window as he mounted the Buckskin and rode off as if the devil himself was after him.

CHAPTER SEVEN

MEREDITH FILLED THE OLD CLAW-FOOTED tub with warm water and carefully stepped in, easing her way down into the mound of bubbles. Placing a folded towel behind her head, she lay back reviewing the past hour in her mind.

There was definitely something going on between Dakota and her, but she wasn't exactly sure what it was. She knew she loved him and always had, but not in *that* way. The sexual tension between them, however, was something she couldn't deny. She had to admit he turned her on in a primal sort of way.

Forty-five minutes later the water had cooled and Meredith began to shiver. She stood and wrapped a towel around her as she stepped out onto the bath mat. Wiping herself dry, she walked into her bedroom.

Opening her suitcase, she hastily rummaged through her clothes. Choosing a pair of blue jeans and a green light-flannel L.L.Bean shirt, she added clean socks and sat down on the edge of the bed, pulling on her cowboy boots. "Wow," she said, tugging on the boots. "These sure are snug. I bet I'll have blisters before the day is out." She stood and stomped about the room, willing the boots to loosen up.

Her brown hair, no longer short and unruly, was now picture perfect; shoulder-length, highlighted and flowing with natural loose curl. Pulling her hair back into a ponytail and securing it with a rubber band, she noticed a few tendrils of curls

35

creeping out around her face as her hair dried. She snorted and let them be.

Never caring much for make-up, she added a bit of blush and a light red lipstick. Surveying herself in the mirror, she decided she looked good enough to go with Gramps on his mystery ride.

Descending the stairs, she heard her grandfather's old truck sputter and come to a halt in the dirt driveway. She shook her head. Why he still drove that old truck was beyond her. He certainly could afford a new one.

Nellie Belle was an old 1948 red Ford. Its fenders and running board nearly rusted through, the visor over the windshield was cracked, and the tailgate had long ago fallen off. The interior was almost as bad as the exterior. The dashboard was faded and cracked and knobs were missing from the radio. Springs were sticking up through the seat's upholstery. Maneuvering for a comfortable spot took some doing.

Two quick raps on the back door and Gramps entered the kitchen. "Meredith. You ready?" he hollered.

"Be right there," she replied.

Gramps, Charlie Parker to his friends, was seventy-nine years old, white-haired, sharp as a tack and bright as a new penny. His wife, Doris, had passed on ten years ago after a long battle with breast cancer. His only daughter, Velvet, had recently succumbed to cirrhosis of the liver, brought on by her many years of drinking.

"By the way, Meredith, I'd like to stop at the General Store on our way."

"Okay, Gramps."

IN RECENT YEARS, CHARLIE had taken a liking to Sadie Abbott, a widow ten years his junior. He had never pursued her out of respect for Velvet, who would have been mortified if her father had begun dating. Now that Velvet was gone, Charlie hoped he might have a chance with Sadie.

Sadie's husband, Cutter, owner of Stony Creek's General Store, died from pneumonia eight years previously leaving lock, stock, and barrel to Sadie.

The only day she closed the store was the day she laid Cutter to rest. Determined to keep the store solvent, she was open seven days a week, just as Cutter had done, even on days when all she wanted to do was stay in bed and grieve for her husband.

Since Velvet's passing, Charlie made daily trips to the General Store. He bought tools, nails, and other assorted items he already owned just to see Sadie and make small talk with her. In her heart, Sadie knew Charlie cared for her, and she was more than smitten with him, too. Knowing he was shy and probably wouldn't have courage to make the first move, she decided to take matters into her own hands.

One afternoon Charlie came into the store while Sadie was sweeping the floor. Looking up at him, she smiled and put the broom down. Wiping her hands on her apron and smoothing back her hair she walked over to him. "Charlie Parker. Would you like to take me to dinner some night?"

Charlie could barely answer, the lump in his throat nearly strangling him. He wiped his brow with the back of his hand and nodded his head up and down like a bobble-head dog in the back window of a car. "Yes, ma'am, I sure would." After their first date, the townsfolk considered them a couple.

"I'M READY GRAMPS," Meredith said as she made her way into the kitchen.

"Well, let's go, then." He opened the kitchen door for her.

Walking out to the driveway, she asked. "Why keep this God-forsaken old truck when you could buy any truck you want?

"I don't want another truck," he said a bit gruffly. "This one runs fine. And besides, she reminds me of your grandmother before she got sick; a little faded on the outside maybe, but devoted to taking care of me."

Lovingly, he rubbed the rusty old fender with his gnarled hand as if he were stroking his wife's arm. His eyes watered and he turned away from Meredith and cleared his throat.

She put her hand on her grandfather's shoulder. "Sorry," she said softly. "That was terribly insensitive of me. I didn't mean to hurt your feelings."

He turned to her and smiled. "Let's say we get the heck out of here and head to town."

Climbing into the cab of the truck, Meredith noticed the driver's seat had a permanent indentation exactly the size of Charlie's butt. She grimaced when she tried to sit down. Wiggling her way around the springs that were precariously sticking through the upholstery, she noticed that her grandfather had covered them in duct tape to keep them from being so sharp. Gramps thought of everything.

A few seconds later Charlie cranked the ignition, put the truck in gear, and they were off. Leaving the driveway, the road became a dirt washboard. "I think the grader will be coming by today," Charlie said as they bumped along.

"I sure hope so," Meredith replied, hanging onto the metal armrest for dear life. "I'm not used to these roads anymore. They're not too good for Mercedes, either."

"Well, old Nellie Belle here doesn't mind them at all, do you Nellie?" he asked, patting the dashboard of the old truck.

Sitting in silence, they made their way to Stony Creek, each lost in their own thoughts. "Watch it, Gramps," Meredith yelled, grabbing him by the arm. *Kerthump!* "Gross! Gramps, you just ran over a big bull snake."

"Hmmm," he said, scratching his head. "I thought it was just a shadow in the road." Looking in the rear view mirror, he saw the snake wriggling slowly into the field. "Didn't kill him. Guess he'll think twice before sunning himself across this road again." Meredith looked over at her grandfather and rolled her eyes.

Turning right onto Main Street, they drove slowly toward the end of town.

Stony Creek was a real turn of the century cowboy town; Doctor's office, General Store, vintage shop, two saloons, drugstore, two banks, western-wear shop, one gas station, an elementary school, and one high school. There were also five churches, a coffee shop, a few specialty shops and a movie theater owned by "out- of- staters." The sidewalks were wooden and hitching posts stood outside of each business. The only traffic light, which blinked yellow, hung over the intersection heading out of town. It was more likely that a person would be struck by a tractor than an automobile in Stony Creek, or run down by a drunken cowboy on a horse. It was picturesque perfect, but Meredith wondered if she would ever feel at ease in this little town where she grew up.

"Gramps, didn't you want to stop at the General Store?"

"We can do that on the way back," he said, driving on through town.

At the intersection, he took a left. A mile down the road he turned into a dirt driveway. "There it is," he said. "It's yours, Meredith. Your mother bought it for you before she died. The land is yours, too."

Staring at the monstrosity in front of her, Meredith was at a loss for words. Finally she spoke. "Was she out of her cotton

Stony Creek Diner

pickin' mind or what?" she exclaimed.

CHAPTER EIGHT

CHARLIE LIFTED HIS BUTT off the truck seat and shoved his hand into the right pocket of his jeans. Retrieving a key that was dangling from a rabbit's foot key chain, he glanced over at Meredith. She hadn't moved a muscle and her mouth was hanging open in shock.

"Darlin', here, take this," he said, passing her the key.

Shaking her head, Meredith still couldn't believe what she was seeing. Sitting on a parcel of unkempt land was an old diner. She'd seen a few diners on the east coast, but never in Montana. Looking at her grandfather, who was still holding the dangling key, she asked, "Where did she find this *thing* and why did she bring it here?"

"She loved you, honey."

"Oh yeah, Gramps, I know how much she loved me. I was always an embarrassment to her and she never let me forget it." Tears spilled out of her eyes and down her face as she continued. "She was a selfish, spoiled woman who only thought of herself. She even drove Daddy away and no one has heard from him in twenty years."

"I know it seems that way, darlin'," Charlie said, patting Meredith on the knee, "but you have no idea how much your mother missed you. She read about this diner in the 'Buy It or Swap It' monthly flyer. She made a few calls and then a special trip to Wyoming to look at it, even when she was so sick. I

41

thought the trip would kill her, but she was determined to go. She bought it on sight, and had it trucked in. Cost her a pretty penny, too. She knew you loved to cook, being a chef and all. Stony Creek only has one café and she thought you might be able to turn this into a profitable business."

"I don't even live here anymore, Gramps," Meredith wailed.

"I know you don't, darlin', but we were hoping that you might want to stay once you saw the diner. Sadly, your mother passed away before she ever got the chance to show it to you."

"I only came home in the first place because you called to tell me that Velvet was really sick and that I should come. Otherwise, I doubt I would have stepped foot in this town again. Then in true Velvet-like fashion and to keep control, she up and died before I got here."

"I think it's time you made peace with the past," Charlie said somewhat gruffly. "I know you had it tough as a child, and for that I'm sorry. But, if you don't let things go, then you'll stay stuck and will never get on with your future."

"How can you say that?" Meredith raised her voice, wiping at her eyes. "I've made a career for myself and I've been quite successful at it, too."

"That's true," Charlie agreed. "However, you've never been married, started a family, or had much of a life outside of being a chef. Time's a fleetin' and you had better think about getting a life."

"Maybe I've never wanted to get married and have a family. Did you ever think of that? Maybe I'm afraid I'll be the type of mother that Velvet was," she cried, "and I wouldn't wish that on any kid. She was a total bitch!"

Charlie turned his head away, drawing in a deep breath. This was the last straw! He was through mollycoddling her.

Instinctively, Meredith knew she had overstepped her

42

bounds and her grandfather was having a difficult time controlling his temper.

Turning back to Meredith, he pointed his finger at her. He didn't try to hide his anger, although he never raised his voice. "I'm only going to say this once. Never call your mother a bad name in my presence again. No matter what she did, and God knows she did a lot of things I didn't like, she was still my daughter and I loved her more than you'll ever imagine." He swallowed a deep sob that threatened to burst forth. Clearing his throat, he grabbed the door handle. "Now let's get out of this truck and take a look at what your mother bought for you."

Meredith didn't say a word and did as her grandfather told her. They walked toward the diner, keeping an eye on the ground for an unwelcome snake or other predator hiding in the bushes. "I think you should take this," Charlie said, holding the key out to Meredith.

She opened her palm and wrapped her fingers around the furry key ring her grandfather placed in her hand. They stood back taking in the scene before them.

The exterior of the 1940s Worcester Semi streamliner was a mess of discolored, banged up stainless steel. Most of the windows were broken. It was apparent that someone had taken pleasure in using the diner for target practice. A Budweiser sign hung haphazardly in one of the windows. The glass in the front door was broken and had been boarded up with plywood. Meredith dreaded going inside.

Together they walked up to the door. Charlie hopped up onto the temporary steps he had placed there earlier. Holding out his hand, Meredith grabbed on and he pulled her onto the steps.

With trepidation, she put the key in the rusty lock and turned it. The door stuck briefly. Charlie covered Meredith's hand with his own and gave it a quick shove. Squeaking loudly as if protesting the invasion, the door opened. Cautiously stepping inside, her grandfather close behind, she was amazed at what she saw.

Above and below the windows, the walls were a lacquered oak accented with Lucite panels which also covered the ceiling. The stainless steel prep area was behind the counter and further back was the kitchen.

A long stone counter with red and white leather stools badly in need of repair stood on one side of the diner; the front of the counter was red and white ceramic tile in an intricate triangle pattern as was the floor below it. Adjacent to the counter were several oak booths with red vinyl backing, taking up the remainder of the space.

Vintage Seeburg Teardrop wall speakers hung at each end of the diner. Beside each booth, attached to the wall, was a small jukebox, just like the ones Meredith had seen back east. For twenty-five cents, you could play five songs and listen while you ate. She was quite sure the jukeboxes no longer worked, but they would make a great conversation piece.

"So, what do you think?" Charlie asked.

Meredith hated to admit it, but she *was* intrigued and wondered if she could actually make it work. That would mean staying in Stony Creek though; something she wasn't sure she could do.

"I kind of like it," she said hesitantly. "It would take a lot of time and money to get it restored. But, since I have the money and the time, I'll think it over."

"Good. I was hoping you'd say that. I've missed you."

Just then, they heard a truck. Looking out through broken blinds hanging askew in the windows, they saw Dakota jump down from his Dodge Ram.

Wearing an olive green vest and blue jeans, a gun strapped to his waist, Meredith recognized Dakota's uniform as that of a Montana Game Warden. How could she not have known anything about him after all these years? Then she remembered. All they'd talked about ever since she came home was her. He hadn't opened up and shared his life at all. Still, Meredith's heart fluttered crazily when she saw him. She hitched up a slipping bra strap and strode across the diner. She needed a minute to calm her nerves.

"Hey," Dakota said, as he stepped inside. He had seen the diner when it arrived the year before and had the same reaction that he expected Meredith did. It wasn't his place to question Velvet's motives, but he secretly hoped that it might bring Meredith back.

"Hey," Charlie and Meredith said at the same time.

"Never saw anything like this before. Very unusual for this part of the country." He glanced around the diner. "So, what do you think about it, Meredith?"

"When did you become a game warden?" she asked, staring at his uniform.

"About fifteen years ago."

Looking over at her grandfather, she frowned. "You're not one for giving out much information, are you?"

"You never asked."

"Doesn't mean I didn't care and wouldn't have wanted to know how he was," she replied, shaking her head in disgust.

"Hel-lo, I'm right here," Dakota broke in, pointing his finger at himself, hoping to distract her from the issue of him being a warden. "I asked you a few minutes ago. What do you think of this place?"

"It's different that's for sure, but I kind of like it. I need some time to think before I decide what I'm going to do. I'll be back there exploring while you men talk," she said, pointing toward the kitchen.

"Better take this." Charlie passed her a flashlight. Meredith walked into the windowless kitchen. A streak of light shined through an exhaust vent in the wall, but otherwise it was completely dark. She shone the flashlight about the room, spotting a large gas stove with grill, an old refrigerator, and a sink. Taking a step forward she stumbled over something on the floor. An icy chill ran down her spine making her call out.

"Gramps, Dakota, get in here!"

Hearing the fear in her voice, they nearly stumbled over each other getting to the kitchen. "What's wrong?" Gramps asked. Dakota protectively put his arm around Meredith, drawing her close to him. He was holding his gun in the other hand ready to shoot an unwanted predator.

"Look at this," she said sharply, shining the flashlight onto the floor. Scattered about the room were blankets, newspapers, and opened cans. "It looks like someone's been staying in here." She leaned against Dakota's chest. Gramps bent down and picked up a newspaper noting the date. "This is yesterday's paper," he grumbled.

CHAPTER NINE

GRAMPS DROPPED MEREDITH OFF at her mother's house before heading back to town to spend some time with Sadie.

Plopping down onto a hassock in the living room, Meredith crossed one leg over the other. Grabbing a boot by the heel and toe, she pulled with all her might to work it off her swollen foot, almost toppling over backwards in the process. With some reluctance and an audible "shit" from Meredith, the boot let go and flew across the room. Taking a big breath, she rested for a moment before tackling the other one. Once done she removed her socks and wiggled her toes to get the blood flowing again.

Looking about the living room, she noticed there were no pictures of her father or her anywhere in sight. In fact, it looked like Velvet had erased any type of past life with them from the room. A few trophies sat on the mantle along with one small framed photo of her grandparents, Charlie and Doris. *Did she really hate us that much or was it her way of coping with the loss that she brought onto herself?*

GROWING UP ON ADJACENT RANCHES, Dallas Banning and Velvet Parker had been friends since they were babies.

Their parents, Jack and Marilyn Banning and Charlie and Doris Parker, had been best friends since high school. They were married in a double wedding ceremony and bought property next

47

to each other. The women became pregnant at about the same time and it was a race to see who would deliver first.

Dallas was the first to arrive and would be the only child Jack and Marilyn would have. Marilyn suffered three subsequent miscarriages before they stopped trying for more children.

As Dallas grew older, he was the picture of his father; dark hair, dark eyes, a handsome face and long muscular legs. At his full height, he was near six feet tall. Dallas, an easy-going child, was the apple of his parents' eyes.

Velvet, on the other hand, came into the world a frail little baby. Since most of their time was spent taking care of their sickly daughter, Charlie and Doris made up their minds not to have more children. Because of their constant doting, Velvet became extremely spoiled and demanding.

She was a beautiful child with long blond hair, sky-blue eyes, and a winning smile. A petite little thing, 'no bigger than a minute' Charlie used to say, and 'smart as whip', too.

Velvet had her father wrapped tightly around her finger. He was unable to say no to her and indulged her every whim. Doris, no match for her strong-willed daughter, didn't have the fortitude to fight with her.

Over the years, Dallas and Velvet spent many a summer's day fishing in the creek and inner tubing on the Madison River. On Velvet's sixteenth birthday, she and Dallas were walking along the bank of the river when she slipped on a loose rock and fell in.

The current was swift and she began to spin away. Dallas, running along beside her yelled, "Hang on Velvet. I'll save you."

Her terror-stricken face encouraged Dallas to run fast. As the current was about to take her around the bend, Dallas reached out and grabbed her by her long hair. Yanking her backward in a desperate attempt to get her close to the shore, she flailed about, grabbing his arm and nearly toppling him into the water with her. But he held fast and soon they were both lying on the bank gasping for air.

Rolling towards him and throwing an arm around his neck, Velvet whispered, "I love you, Dallas. You saved my life."

"I've *always* loved you, Velvet." He leaned over her, brushed her wet hair back from her face, and shyly lowered his mouth to hers. It was their first kiss, but only the first of many kisses to come. From that day forward, they were inseparable.

THE PARKERS AND THE BANNINGS were organizers of the once-a-year Stony Creek Rodeo. To ensure that the children were expert riders they were introduced to the saddle and riding before they were a year old. Knowing how to ride was a necessity on a working ranch, but they also wanted the children involved in the rodeo scene they loved.

As soon as the children were old enough to ride by themselves, they participated in the Fourth of July and rodeo parades. In their teens, they became contestants. Velvet earned her fame as a barrel racer and was crowned Miss Teen Rodeo Montana. Dallas was a bull rider winning scores of blue ribbons, trophies, and belt buckles. Between the two of them, they were unbeatable. For five years, they held the title of King and Queen of the rodeo.

Following their high school graduation, they were married during intermission at the Stony Creek Rodeo. The whole county showed up for the big event.

After the wedding, they traveled the rodeo circuit, going from state to state winning large purses and living a carefree life. When they needed a break, they made their way home to Montana for a visit with their parents.

Three years later, Dallas wanted to quit the circuit and put down roots, but Velvet refused. "If you want to quit, go ahead," she told him. "You can go home, but I'm staying with the rodeo. I might even find someone who will appreciate me for who I am."

Velvet knew her threats would get to Dallas and if she pouted long enough she would get her way.

He gave in as he always did and things went along pretty much the same for the next year …that is, until Velvet got pregnant with Meredith.

CHAPTER TEN

VELVET STORMED INTO THEIR TRAVEL TRAILER making as much noise as she possibly could and slammed the door shut. The doctor had given her devastating news, and she was mad as a hornet. Stamping her feet down the tiny hallway, she entered the bedroom where Dallas was just waking from an afternoon nap.

"Hey, Babe," he said, rousing himself to a half-sitting position.

"Don't you 'hey babe me,'" she screamed, slapping him full-force in the face.

"What the hell is the matter with you?" he hollered, rubbing the telltale welt, the size of his wife's hand, on his flame-red cheek.

"I'll tell you what the matter with me is," she yelled, drawing her hand back and feigning another slap to his face.

Wincing he started to stand up, but she shoved him hard, toppling him back onto the bed. She loomed over him, all five feet of her, shaking her clenched fists in his face.

"How dare you! How dare you!" Looking around she spotted her pocketbook, picked it up and threw it at him.

Ducking to fend off the flying purse, he jumped up and grabbed her by the wrists. "What? What did I do?"

"How dare you get me pregnant! You did this on purpose so we'd have to leave the rodeo," she cried.

51

"You're pregnant?"

"Yes, I'm pregnant," she shrieked. "The doctor says I'm about ten weeks. It's not too late for me to get rid of it, but he says you'll need to sign a consent form since it's your baby, too."

Reaching into the purse on the bed where it landed, she retrieved the paperwork and handed it to Dallas. Her wrath subsided for the moment; she begged, "Please, honey, sign this paper for me."

"I'm not signing anything," Dallas said, shaking his head.

"You have to sign it," Velvet whined. "I'm not ready to be a mother. In fact, I never wanted to have a baby. You're the one that wanted children."

"That's right, Velvet, I do. We are *not* getting rid of this baby," he said.

"Then I'll find someone who will perform the abortion, with or without you," she said defiantly.

"If you do that," he threatened, pointing his finger at her, "I'll divorce you. I'll tell everyone who will listen why I got rid of you just like you want to get rid of our baby. I'm sure your parents would be happy to learn that their daughter aborted the grandchild they've been hoping for."

He threw his arms up totally disgusted and paced around the room, anger boiling inside him. His love for Velvet was so strong he couldn't imagine life without her, but at this very moment he hated her and everything she stood for. His feelings were raw and he resisted the urge to hit her. He stopped pacing, crossed his arms and boldly met her gaze.

"Since you're almost three months along you shouldn't be barrel racing anymore. We're going to quit the circuit *now*, and head back to Stony Creek."

"Ha," she snorted. "I don't think so."

"Oh yes we are Velvet. I've always let you do whatever you wanted, but this time we're doing it my way. I'll get the trailer ready and we'll head out this evening."

"I can't believe you're serious about this," Velvet gulped, in between loud sobs.

"You had better believe it," Dallas warned, "because it's what we're going to do."

Latching the cupboard doors and closets, throwing pots and pans under the sink, he started readying the trailer for its move. Tossing and slamming things around made him feel good. It kept him from slapping his wife and doing something he knew he'd regret later on.

Dallas opened the trailer door and was about to go outside when he felt Velvet's hand on his shoulder. He turned and looked at her. Tears streaming down her face she looked so sad.

He couldn't help himself. He turned and embraced her, kissing her deeply, giving in to the desire he felt for his wife. Velvet did not resist him. He picked her up and carried her down the hallway to their bedroom. Their lovemaking was passionate and wild, more so than it had been in a long time. When it was over, they lay back, spent, yet still clinging to each other. With her mouth near his ear, she whispered, "Dallas, are you sure you won't sign those papers for me?"

He couldn't believe what she was saying. He shoved her away from him with such force she nearly fell out of bed.

"Dallas, wait," she said, putting her hand out to stop him. Pushing her away, he jumped up, grabbed his pants, and ran out of the room. His emotions were a jumble of pent up anger and frustration; his heart pounded rapidly. He staggered, as if drunk, and fell to his knees, deep sobs wracking his body. He knew at that moment his life would never be the same. *That was a*

53

mighty low blow, Velvet. I don't know if I'll ever forgive you for that.

They left for Stony Creek that evening. Silence filled the air on the long trek to Montana and the rift between Dallas and Velvet was ever widening.

SIX MONTH'S LATER, during Montana's worst blizzard in thirty years, Meredith Parker Banning quietly made her way into the world, barely mewing after she was delivered from her mother. She lay on the bed next to Velvet, eyes squinting at the harsh light in the room. There was no hospital bed for this delivery. Because of the severity of the storm, Meredith came into the world with the help of Anna Morgan as midwife.

"Velvet, look at the baby, please," Dallas pleaded.

"Take her away," Velvet snapped, turning her back on her baby. "She just about killed me."

Anna picked Meredith up and wrapped her in a soft pink blanket. She smiled and placed her in her daddy's arms. Looking down at his baby daughter, his heart filled with a love like never before.

"Happy Birthday, little girl," he whispered, placing the most gentle kiss on her forehead.

Meredith's lashes fluttered at the sound of her father's voice and she opened her eyes. Dallas felt she was looking directly into his soul and they became one. He traced her face with his fingertip feeling the soft down on her cheeks. When he touched her chin, her little hand grabbed his finger and she held on tight.

DALLAS AND VELVET'S MARRIAGE had been in name only since the day he insisted she have their baby and return to Montana. Living for his daughter and protecting her from Velvet's wrath kept him going for years.

One year to the day that Meredith left home, so did Dallas. He still loved his wife, but she wanted nothing to do with him.

His parents, Jack and Marilyn, were killed in a plane crash a few years earlier while on a cattle buying trip so there was no reason for him to stay. No one had heard from him in years.

Velvet, not having a clue why everyone would leave her, became bitter and withdrawn blaming Meredith and Dallas for her miseries. She turned to the bottle as a means of escape. While waiting for them to admit they were wrong and come crawling back to her, she drowned herself in the finest bourbon available.

CHAPTER ELEVEN

CHARLIE PULLED "NELLIE BELLE" INTO a parking spot in front of Sadie Abbot's general store. He had planned to stop by and see her earlier, but time spent at the diner with Meredith had taken up most of the afternoon.

Stepping up onto the wooden sidewalk, he walked the few feet to the store, and turned the brass handle on the door. A soft bell hanging by a string announced his arrival.

"Be right there," Sadie hollered from somewhere in the back. "Have a look around."

Charlie took in his surroundings, always amazed at what she had done with the general store since her husband's death. Sadie had divided it into two separate shops; one filled with vintage items and the other general merchandise. The store was nothing like this when her late husband, Cutter, was alive.

A year after Cutter's passing, a shop on the other side of the general store went out of business and Sadie snatched it up. She hired carpenters to knock down a connecting wall, install shelving, and had the entire place painted.

While the carpenters were at work, Sadie went on scavenger hunts for items she remembered when she was a child. She knew Cutter would never have allowed her to take on such a venture, but Cutter wasn't here anymore and she could do

56

what she pleased. She was full of anticipation that her idea would be successful, and within a few months, her new store was in operation.

From the time the doors opened, the locals and tourists told her how much they loved the vintage shop. It took them back in time and rejuvenated old memories.

The highlight for both adults and children were the glass-fronted candy cases stocked with Mary Janes, Root Beer barrels, Sugar Daddy's, Tootsie Rolls, little wax soda bottles filled with fruit juice, and big red wax lips. Black Jack, Teaberry and Bazooka Bubble Gum were all-time favorites, too. Back when Charlie was a boy, he remembered buying them for a penny. Sadie sold them for five-cents apiece.

Large glass jars filled with Jaw Breakers, a round hard candy in different fruit flavors, sat beside the candy case.

At the end of the counter were rows of rhinestone rings, sparkling in black velvet trays. Little girls were drawn to the rings and many bought their first "diamond" for $1.25.

Young girls also loved the paper dolls and coloring books displayed on a circular metal rack. Boys liked the comic books that ranged from Donald Duck to X-Men.

The store was a child's haven and an adult's stroll down memory lane, especially seeing the stocked shelves with playing cards and Sparklers. Looms were available for weaving colorful potholders. Other reminders of the days gone by were Pick-Up-Sticks, Checkers and small plastic birds in a variety of colors that would chirp when filled with water and blown into.

A dented green metal wash bucket filled with ice and bottles of Nehi orange and grape soda and Coca-Cola sat near the front door. Just outside on the sidewalk was a Bucking Bronco that the children could ride for twenty-five cents.

The tinkle of the bell announced another customer and Charlie glanced at the door. *A tourist,* he thought, noting the city-slicker way she was dressed in high heels and blue jeans. *That just ain't right.* He shook his head and looked away.

Sadie came out from the back. Smiling, she nodded at Charlie, and spoke to the woman. "Welcome to Cutters General Store and Vintage Shop. Please, take your time and look around. If you need groceries or other provisions, they're in the general store." She pointed the way.

She turned her attention back to Charlie. "What a pleasant surprise. I was hoping you'd stop in today. I haven't seen you in a bit."

"As you know, Meredith is here. I took her out to the diner this morning."

"Hmmm, what did she think?"

"I'm not sure. At first, she couldn't believe her eyes, but when we got inside, I think she rather liked it. I have no idea though if she'll stay and try to make it work."

"I hope she will. It's time she came home. Dakota's been waiting a long time."

"Yeah, I know. He won't wait forever though. He's loved her since he was a boy."

"Do you think she has any idea how he feels?" She glanced over at the customer who was browsing the aisles, then turned her attention back to Charlie.

"Right now she's so mad at her mother that I don't think she feels or knows much else. By the way, looks like a squatter's been sleeping in the diner at night. Have you seen anyone around lately that doesn't belong?"

"I haven't, but I'll pass the word and keep my eyes open."

"How much is this?" the woman asked, holding out a book of Shirley Temple paper dolls. "I haven't seen paper dolls like these since I was a child."

Sadie turned her attention to her customer and smiled.

"Aren't they great? They're $2.00."

"Are you sure? You're not going to make any money at this price."

"My store prices aren't that unusual. I think most owners of vintage shops aren't in it for the money. Originally, I got the idea when I was traveling down south and had lunch at a Cracker Barrel Restaurant and General Store. I fell in love with the concept and before I knew it this store became my hobby. I have so much fun picking out the items I want to sell."

"I have a few more items here, too," the woman said. She walked toward Sadie, carefully holding her purchases as if they were priceless antiques. "I'm ready to check out."

"Follow me, please." Sadie led the way to a wooden counter where a vintage National Cash Register with clamshell inlay stood proud like a peacock.

"What a beautiful cash register," the woman remarked, running her hand along the sleek polished wood.

"Yes, she sure is a beauty. Come closer and see the carved lid with "Jefferson Market" on it.

"I love it," the woman exclaimed. "In fact, I love this whole store. I'm going to tell all my friends when they're in the area they must stop in. You don't happen to sell any of these items online do you?"

"I'm sorry, I don't. I have all I can do to keep both these stores running every day. If I got involved with the computer, too, I wouldn't have a minute to myself."

Sadie added up the woman's purchases on a small calculator carefully hidden out of sight. "Your items come to $6.10." Pressing the $5, $1, and ten-cent keys a bell rang and the money drawer opened. The woman stood there grinning.

"This is the neatest thing I've ever seen. I hope you never close this store, and you really should go online you know."

"Thank you. I plan to keep the store open for a long time.

I really enjoy doing this, but I don't want it to become a job. When it does, then I'll have to close. This is for fun and I want to keep it that way."

"I can understand that," the woman said. She gave Sadie a small wave of her hand and walked out the door. "I'll be back," she promised.

"Charlie, are you still here?" Sadie called out.

"I'm here," he answered, wandering out of the general store and back to Sadie, a small brown paper bag in his hand. "I needed some ten-penny nails. Thought I'd go get them while you were busy with your customer."

"I'm glad you didn't leave," she said a bit flirtatiously, a big smile on her face.

Charlie's heart did a flip-flop, her smile grabbing him right in the belly. "I was wondering if you'd like to have supper with me tonight. The Powder Horn Café has prime rib on special."

"Sounds good, but I have a better idea. Why don't you come to my house instead? I made an elk stew yesterday. It'll be real tasty after sitting over night. I'll even throw in some buttermilk biscuits."

Charlie's mouth watered with anticipation of the hearty stew, along with the excitement of spending a whole evening with Sadie. He felt like he was sixteen again. "It'd be a pleasure to have dinner with you, Sadie. Can I bring anything?"

"Just bring yourself," she said. "Oh, should we invite Meredith?"

"Heck no," he said, grinning from ear to ear. "I think Meredith will be just fine. She don't need to tag along on her granddaddy's date with the prettiest lady in town."

"Oh, Charlie," Sadie fussed, obviously embarrassed by his remarks, but flattered at the same time. Her late husband, Cutter, had never been one to show much attention or affection, even though she knew he loved her. This was all new for Sadie and she was thoroughly enjoying it.

"Shall we say six-o-clock?" she asked.

"Don't you keep the store open until seven?"

"I do, but I recently hired Gage Boone to work for me after school. He closes for me, too, when I have plans. So far, he's working out fine and seems to be a nice hard-working boy."

"That's good, Sadie. You were working way too much anyway." Charlie placed his Stetson on his head, gave Sadie a quick hug, and headed for the door. Turning, he smiled. "See you at six."

"I'm looking forward to it."

Not as much as I am, Charlie thought, jumping off the wooden sidewalk onto the dirt like a teenage boy. *I'd hop up and click my heels if I didn't think I'd fall on my danged fool face.*

CHAPTER TWELVE

TAYLOR BOONE WAS IN A FOUL MOOD. Waking up before dawn in his truck, covered in his own vomit, was not the way he wanted to start his day. His head pounded and he needed to take a leak.

Grabbing the door handle, he pushed it down. The door creaked and opened a crack, but then stuck. Pushing against it with his shoulder, it still wouldn't budge. Spewing several four-letter words, he lay back on the seat. Hanging onto the steering wheel for leverage, he kicked the door with both feet as hard as he could before it flew open.

Staggering out of the truck, he made his way 'round to the side. He unzipped his fly and urinated on the back tire, much like a hound dog marking his territory.

He was furious at Carrie for leaving him in the truck all night. As soon as he got in the house, she was going to pay.

Half-drunk, he weaved his way up the steps to their trailer home, hanging onto the railing. He tried the door. It was locked. He banged loudly, the sound of metal reverberating throughout the park they lived in.

"Carrie. Open this fucking door," he yelled, banging it with both fists and giving it a hard kick.

One by one, neighbors turned on lights and opened their doors to the ruckus. "Taylor, keep it down out there. Some of us are still sleeping, or we were."

"Screw you," Taylor yelled back, giving his neighbor the finger. Turning his attention back to the door he banged again. "Carrie, you better open this door or you're gonna' get it," he threatened.

Carrie knew that she was in big trouble the minute she decided to leave Taylor in the truck for the night. She hadn't slept a wink. Fearing that he would come in and beat her or worse yet, take his rage out on one of the boys, she had locked the door hoping it would give her an advantage.

Nervously she made her way towards the bellowing and pounding. Eighteen-year-old Gage met her in the hallway. "Go back to bed," she demanded.

"But, Ma," he protested.

Taking him by the shoulders, she turned him toward the bedrooms. "Back to bed, Gage. I mean it. Take care of your brothers. I'll be okay."

Carrie turned the dead bolt and backed away. "It's unlocked, Taylor," she said, her heart thumping wildly.

The door flew open and Carrie raised both hands to protect herself from her husband's wrath. Not quick enough, she felt his fist strike the side of her head and his knee connect with her stomach. She went down onto the floor, fighting for air that had been knocked out of her. She grabbed her stomach with one hand and covered her head with the other to ward off more blows. "Taylor, please stop!" she pleaded.

"I'll teach you never to lock me out of my house again," he hollered, grabbing a handful of her hair and pulling her to an upright position. He drew back his hand to hit her again when Gage's fist came out of nowhere and smashed into Taylor's half-mended nose.

"Son of a bitch," he yelled, blood spurting down his face. Stunned by the unexpected blow and before he had a chance to react, Gage grabbed his father around the neck, opened the door and viciously threw him down the steps like a sack of trash. Grabbing a 12-gauge shotgun off the gun rack by the door, he pointed it at Taylor who was sprawled on his back in the yard.

"Don't you move," he yelled. Tears streamed down his face and he yelled again. "Don't you move or I'll shoot you right between the eyes. If you ever hit Ma again, I'll kill you."

Taylor started to get up. "You hold on a minute, son, or you'll be getting it next."

"I told you, Dad. Stay where you are or I'll shoot you." He released the safety.

Carrie picked herself up off the floor. "Gage, Gage," she cried out grabbing his arm. "Don't do it. Give me the gun."

"Ma, you stay back." Gage brushed her away. "He's never going to hurt you again."

Seventeen-year-old Dusty appeared with his arms around his nine-year-old brother, Danny, who was crying. Gage had made him promise to stay in the bedroom and take care of their little brother. "I called the Sheriff and Grandpa, too," Dusty said to Gage.

Hearing a siren in the background, Taylor thought about getting up. Looking at the gun pointed at his head and seeing Gage's face and the rage in his eyes, he knew that his kid meant business so he stayed put. Within minutes, Sheriff George Logan pulled into the yard. Seeing Gage inside the open doorway with a gun, George cautiously stepped outside his vehicle, holster unsnapped and ready. *Please, God. Don't make me have to shoot this boy.*

"What's going on here?" he asked, his voice non-threatening. He noticed that Taylor was lying on the ground with a bloody nose and a 12-gauge pointed at his head. *It's about time someone knocked him on his ass,* he thought.

"Everything's okay, George," Carrie called out, straightening her clothes and using her hands as a comb for her hair.

"Ma, it's not okay," Gage cried, blinking back tears. "We can't live here any longer or he'll end up killing you. When is enough going to be enough? I have a job now. I can take care of you."

Carrie's heart broke, knowing she had placed such a burden on her sons by staying with their father.

"Gage, give me the shotgun," George ordered, holding out his hand and walking up the steps to the trailer.

Carrie put her arm around her son. "Give George the gun, Gage," she said, gently rubbing his back. "Make sure you put the safety back on."

George reached inside the door and took it from the boy's hand.

"Thanks." He turned and went back down the steps to where Taylor was lying.

"You hit her, Taylor?" George asked.

"The bitch deserved it. She locked me out of my own house. Bet she'll think 'fore she does that again. Ain't that right, Carrie?" He glared at his wife.

A red pickup, horn blaring and churning up dust as it pulled into the yard, came to a screeching halt. The door opened and Carrie's father, Larry Owens, shotgun in his hands, stomped over to Taylor who was still on the ground. He pointed the gun directly at him.

From the look of sheer hatred on Larry's face and staring into the double barrel of a shotgun, Taylor pissed his pants, even though he had taken a leak less than an hour before. He felt the warm liquid run down his leg. The front of his jeans turned a dark blue for all the neighbors to witness. This was not a good day for Taylor. Not many men had a gun pointed at their head, but two guns on the same day? Now that was a bit much. He prayed that Larry didn't have an itchy trigger finger.

"Hold on there a minute, Larry," Sheriff Logan ordered. "There's not going to be any shooting here today, unless I'm the one doing the shooting."

"Look at my daughter, George," Larry pointed at Carrie. "One of these days we'll all be too late. I'd rather put this drunken bastard out of his misery now before he beats my daughter to death."

"You're not going to put anyone out of their misery. We'll let the law handle that. I'm going to arrest him and take him in. Don't make me take you, too."

Walking over to Taylor, Sheriff Logan pulled him onto his feet by the front of his shirt. He handcuffed one wrist and twisted his arm behind him. He did the same with the other. Now that he had Taylor secured he read him his rights.

"Taylor Boone, you're under arrest for domestic abuse. Anything you say can and will be used against you in a court of law. You have the right to speak to an attorney. If you can't afford an attorney, one will be appointed to you. Do you understand these rights?"

"Yeah. Just get me the hell out of here and away from all these crazy people."

"We're leaving now," George said, herding Taylor into the back seat of his car.

"Owwww. What the hell?"

"Whoops, Taylor, didn't mean for you to bump your head so hard. You should have ducked down a little more." He turned and winked at Larry.

Watching the Sheriff's car drive out of sight Carrie let loose with a torrent of tears. Only then did she notice her neighbors watching and waiting to see what was going to happen next. "Why don't you all go home now," Larry shouted.

Slowly the crowd dispersed, complaining to each other about the early hour they were roused from their beds.

Hugging his daughter, Larry let Carrie cry her heart out. When she was spent, he said gently, "Pack up your things, Carrie. You, too, boys. You will never spend another night in this house as long as I'm alive. I promise. You're coming home with me and Grandma for a while."

CHAPTER THIRTEEN

SITTING ON THE PORCH in her grandmother's rocking chair, a cup of hot coffee between her hands, Meredith looked toward the west. She watched as the sun slid behind the mountains, leaving glorious colors of red, orange, and yellow in its wake.

The sounds of small animals scurrying through the underbrush settling in for the night gave her a sense of belonging. But did she want to belong? It had been a long day and she had much to think about.

Meredith had been back in Stony Creek for a little over a month. She'd buried her mother and spent time with her grandfather. It was time to decide whether to go back to Florida or stay and try to make a go of it with that stupid diner her mother had left her. She still couldn't believe Velvet had done that. She knew Gramps wanted her to stay, that was a given. She was pretty sure Dakota did, too, although he hadn't come right out and asked her. He probably wouldn't either after the way she had left him high and dry twenty years ago.

The phone rang and she ran inside to answer it. "Hello."

"Hi, Meredith. It's Russ. How's things going out there in no man's land?"

Meredith chuckled at Russ's description of Montana. He had never traveled further north than Ocala. Russell Collins, a native Floridian, was owner of The Grappling Hook, a prestigious seafood restaurant in Key West where Meredith was an executive chef.

"Hi, Russ, great to hear from you. I'm doing okay, and yourself?"

"Doing just fine here. Listen, I know this has been a difficult time for you, but we're getting really busy. I need you to come back. When do you think you'll be ready?"

Meredith had been anticipating his call and knew she'd have to give Russ an answer soon.

"I've taken care of my mother's estate, but I still have a few personal things I need to attend to. Can I give you an answer in …no, wait a minute, Russ. I can give you an answer now."

"What are you saying, Meredith?"

With a sick feeling in the pit of her stomach along with a sense of excitement and anticipation of the future, the words spewed forth before she had a chance to change her mind.

"I've decided to stay here in Stony Creek. Gramps is getting older and has no one but me. I have unfinished work here and, believe it or not, a project on the back burner. My mother bought me a beat up old diner and I'm going to turn it into something that no one in these parts has ever seen."

"Are you sure you know what you're doing?" Russ asked.

"Not really, but I'm going to stick my neck out and give it a try. I've been hiding for twenty years. It's time for me to see what I'm really made of."

"If that's your decision then I wish you all the luck in the world. If for some reason it doesn't work out, you'll always have a job working for me."

"Thanks. I really appreciate that. I'll come back to Florida next week and work out a notice, or stay until you find someone else to take my place," Meredith offered.

"You don't have to do that. Just allow me to use your famous lobster mac and cheese recipe in my restaurant and we'll call it square."

"You got it. I'll put it in writing."

"What are you going to do about your condo?"

"I suppose at some point I'll have to come back and put it on the market. For now though, I'm going to leave things as they are and deal with closing it up later on."

"Well, if there's anything you want me to do to help, just say the word."

"I will, Russ, and thanks so much for everything."

After a few more pleasantries, they said their good-byes with promises to keep in touch.

Meredith roamed around the vast living room. "I can't believe I just did that!" she said, slapping herself on both sides of her head. She realized she was smiling and for the life of her didn't know why. A weight seemed to have lifted off her shoulders and for the first time in a long time, she felt happy.

Picking up the phone and glancing at the clock, she dialed Dakota's number. It was only eight so she knew he hadn't turned in for the night. On the second ring, he picked up.

"Hello."

His deep husky voice made Meredith's knees feel wobbly. "Hey," she said.

Dakota's heart skipped a beat when he heard her voice. "Hey, yourself."

"Want to come over for some coffee and talk?"

"What do you want to talk about?" he asked gruffly. He wasn't about to give in too easily, but he'd already grabbed his boots and was hopping about the room pulling one on and then the other.

"Dakota," she said sternly. "I have something important I

want to discuss with you. Now, are you going to say yes or make me beg?"

"Begging sounds good, but since I doubt you'd really do it, then yes, I'll be over. Give me about fifteen minutes or so."

"See you then." Hanging up the phone and clasping both hands over her head she said, "I think I've just lost my mind." Meredith put on a fresh pot of coffee and went outside to wait for Dakota. Her muscles ached from being tense. Sitting down on the stoop, she rolled her shoulders forward to get the kinks out. She shook her head back and forth. "I hope I haven't made the wrong decision."

She had a habit of second-guessing and over-thinking things, something she hated about herself. As much as she tried to rid herself of anxieties leftover from years of living with Velvet, they often came back to make her question what she knew was right. "What's done is done and I'm going to make the best of it."

Ten minutes later she heard Dakota's truck coming down the driveway. She looked up as he pulled to a stop in front of the porch and let himself out of the cab. His tight-fitting Levi's, jean shirt and leather vest made him look like a model out of a magazine. She sucked in a deep breath and felt a warm, tingly feeling in places she had forgotten about.

Meredith sat with her hands between her knees, and let out a quiet sigh. "Hi," she said smiling. "Want a cup of coffee?"

Dakota nodded. Looking at Meredith and seeing her discomfort made him uneasy. Had she made a decision to leave?

"Do you want to sit on the porch or go inside?" she asked.

"Doesn't matter." He stepped onto the porch. "Can I help?"

She shook her head. "I think we'll sit out here then. I'll

get the coffee. You take yours black, right?

"Right."

"I'll be back in a minute." Meredith retrieved a mug from the cupboard and placed it and her cup on a small wooden tray. She filled the cups with the steaming black liquid and placed four chocolate chip cookies on a small plate.

Making her way to the porch, she used her foot to kick the screen door open and caught it with her butt so it wouldn't slam. She placed the tray on a small table between the two rocking chairs.

"Have a seat." She motioned towards one of the rockers.

Dakota sat down, still not speaking, but eyeing Meredith cautiously.

The silence was broken only by the sound of a lone coyote calling for his mate and the occasional hoot of an owl.

"You are making me so nervous, Dakota. Can't you at least say something?"

"You're the one who asked me over to talk. So talk."

"You don't have to be so nasty about it," she said sarcastically, plopping down into a rocker. She picked up her coffee and took a swallow. "I've made a decision."

"What kind of decision?" he asked. His gut wrenched fearing that she was going to leave again.

"My boss called me from Florida this evening," she rocked back and forth. "He told me he needed me to come back. They're getting really busy."

Dakota's hands tightened around his coffee mug and he took in a quick breath. He hoped Meredith didn't notice. "So, what did you tell him?"

"At first I told him I needed a few more days. Before I finished telling him why I needed more time, I changed my mind. I told him I was going to stay in Stony Creek and open up a diner."

Dakota let his breath out, not realizing he had been holding it. He closed his eyes and leaned his head back, brows drawn together in a frown. Eyes still closed he asked, "Are you positive this is what you want to do? Have you discussed it with your granddad yet?"

"No, I haven't told Gramps yet. I wanted you to be the first to know."

"Why?"

"Dammit Dakota, isn't my staying a good enough reason? I was hoping you were going to be happy that I wasn't going to leave, but oh, no, you have to put me through twenty questions."

"I've only asked you three questions," he snarled. "Quit exaggerating."

"Will you look at me?" she asked.

He turned his head to the side and met her eyes. *God she was beautiful and he loved her so much. He wasn't sure how he was going to manage if she lived in the same town. It was easier having her across the country so he didn't have to see her.* "What do you want from me?"

"I want us to be best friends again. I want you to be glad that I'm going to live here and start a business. I want you to support me in this venture. Can you do that, Dakota?"

"I suppose we can be friends and, of course, I'll support you in your business venture. You're taking on a lot. I hope you're ready for all the hard work it will take to salvage the diner."

"I know it's a big challenge, but I'm up for it. I plan to ask Anna to be one of my cooks, if she might consider coming out of retirement and going to work again."

"Well, that's between you and my mom. I'm not getting in the middle of that."

"Would you go to the diner with me tomorrow? I want to take a good hard look at it, do some measuring, and decide who to hire to refurbish it."

He nodded. "I can go tomorrow morning, but I won't be available for the rest of the week. I have to go up north. There's been some poaching going on. Another ranger is going with me in case there's trouble."

"Please be careful. I'm glad you won't be alone. So, what time tomorrow?"

"How about eight? Maybe we can grab some breakfast after."

"I'd like that."

Checking his watch, Dakota hoisted himself out of the rocker. "It's nearly eleven so I should go. Thanks for the coffee. By the way, I'm glad you're staying."

Meredith felt a rush of happiness. She stopped rocking and got up, walking over to where Dakota was standing. "It'll be alright, Dakota, you'll see." She put her arms around his waist and lay her head on his warm chest.

He stood there, ramrod still, until his arms circled her body with a will of their own. He groaned and embraced her tightly. She stared up at him and his lips found hers in a passionate kiss that left them both weak-kneed. Dakota pushed Meredith away from him and jumped off the porch.

"I'll see you tomorrow morning." He hopped into the cab of his truck, started it up, and with a quick wave took off down the driveway. She watched until the red taillights were out of sight.

Meredith stood there for several more minutes. There was no mistaking that the chemistry between them was magnetic. She was drawn to him like a moth to a flame. She imagined making love to him, remembering the feel of having his body close to hers. Dangerous thoughts, but enticing at the same time.

CHAPTER FOURTEEN

SHERIFF GEORGE LOGAN PULLED his cruiser into the parking lot of Doc Webster's office.

"What we stopping here for?" Taylor asked.

"I want to make sure none of your brains fell out when you hit your head a while back. Just covering my ass."

The sheriff got out and opened the back door of the cruiser. Reaching in, he put his hand on Taylor's head. "Come on out now. Easy does it."

"Am I going to jail?"

"'Fraid so. One of these days you're going to learn to keep your fists to yourself."

Taylor, nearly sober, felt like death warmed over. His tongue was thick, his teeth slimy and his breath foul. He had a bitch of a hangover, too. Rolling his head around he tried to get the crick out of his neck left by sleeping in the truck all night. Hurting everywhere, he felt like a stampede of buffalo had run over him and crapped in his mouth. His nose was broken, his kid had thrown him down the steps into the yard nearly breaking every bone in his body, or so it felt like. Adding insult to injury, he cracked his head getting into the cruiser. *This is going to be a long day,* he thought.

The hour was early and a *Closed* sign was in the window of the doc's office. Everyone in Stony Creek knew that the sign was just a formality and no one would ever be turned away regardless of the hour.

Sheriff Logan pulled Taylor around to the side of the building and knocked on the back door.

"Will you take these cuffs off me?" Taylor asked, wiggling his arms behind him. "I ain't gonna' do nothin', I promise."

Sheriff Logan squinted his eyes as he looked at Taylor. "Doc has a couple of kids inside. I'm not sure I can trust you."

"I promise, Sheriff. My arms are breaking and so is my back. I'm all done being an ass for one day."

The sheriff thought for a minute before walking behind Taylor and unlocking the cuffs. "Don't make me have to shoot you in front of those kids," he warned, "because I will if you give me a reason."

"I'll be a good boy," he mocked. "I'm fine. Really." He rubbed his wrists.

ELLIOTT WEBSTER WAS TALL, blond, athletic and easy on the eyes. After finishing medical school at Philadelphia College of Osteopathic Medicine, he searched around for a small town to work in for three years to fulfill a scholarship obligation. The school listed several small towns needing a doctor and Elliott needed one of the towns.

Stony Creek caught his eye. The town had been without a doctor for a year and was desperate. Elliott applied for the job. A week later, Mayor Howard Jasper invited Elliott, his wife, Lynda, and their twin sons, David and Douglas, to visit Stony Creek.

A walk down main street was all it took for Elliott to realize this was the type of town where he wanted to practice medicine and raise his sons.

Lynda, on the other hand, wasn't so sure. She was a city

girl and there was nothing in this rinky-dink town for her to do. Where would she shop? How could she possibly make friends with *these* people?

The towns' people, excited at the prospect of having a doctor, threw Elliott and his family a picnic at Bucks Hill State Park. Everyone came from miles around to greet the new doctor and his wife.

Elliott was surprised, but pleased when a woman came up to him and asked for his advice. "Doc, would you mind taking a look at this rash on my arm?"

Lynda rolled her eyes, thinking how rude this woman was.

That evening, after a full day meeting the people of Stony Creek, their bellies full of BBQ, Elliott, Lynda and the boys settled in for the night at the Powder Horn Hotel.

"I really like this town," Elliott gushed. Smiling at his wife he asked, "So what do you think?"

"I'm not sure I can live here," she answered. "There's nothing to do. Shopping is miles away, and I'd be leaving all my friends."

"Won't you at least give it a try?" he pouted like a small child. "For me? It's only three years and if you want to leave after that then I promise, we'll leave."

"Where are we supposed to live?"

"The Mayor told me that the job comes with a house which is also used as the office. All we have to pay is utilities."

"So where's this house?"

"It's located at the end of Main Street. The boys are asleep and I think they'd be safe if we took a walk down there. How about it?"

"I'm not about to leave my children in some fleabag hotel by themselves, and anyway, I'm tired. You can show me in the morning." She walked into the bathroom and slammed the door.

"We have to give them an answer in two days," he hollered to the closed door.

Silence.

IT HAD BEEN THREE YEARS since Doc and his family moved to Stony Creek. The boys were now five years old and would be starting school in the fall.

Lynda hated the isolation and rural life. She never accepted the town or the people, even though the women went out of their way to make her feel welcome. After a year, she left Elliott and the boys and went back East.

THE SHERIFF KNOCKED ON the kitchen door. Elliott was making breakfast for the twins. "Hold on. I'll be right there," he said, wiping his hands on a dishtowel.

He opened the door to find Sheriff Logan and a disheveled-looking Taylor Boone standing on the doorstep.

"Hey, Sheriff. What can I do for you?"

"Taylor here got a nasty lump on his head. I was wondering if you could take a quick look at it. I didn't know if he might need stitches or something.

"Sure. Come on in." Elliott led them through the kitchen and into the office across the hall. The boys were at the table eating their cereal. Dave and Doug looked wide-eyed at Taylor. "It's okay, boys," he reassured his sons. "Mr. Boone won't hurt you. Why don't you hop up here, Taylor?" Elliott patted the examination table.

"I don't think I'll be hopping anywhere today, Doc. Mind if I lay down? I feel a little woozy."

"Sure. How'd you get the lump?"

"I hit my head getting into the cruiser. It didn't hurt at first, but it does now. Do I need stitches?" he asked, rubbing his hand through his hair. "I hate needles."

Elliott looked through Taylor's hair and felt the lump, about the size of a walnut. Parting the hair and peering closer he noticed the skin wasn't broken.

He patted Taylor on the shoulder. "You're fine. No stitches. I suggest you put an ice pack on it when you get home."

"He's not going home," Sheriff Logan said. "I'll make sure he's taken good care of when I lock him up. Thanks, Doc."

"Glad to help," Elliott said.

"Let's go, Taylor," the sheriff said, taking him by the arm and pulling him into a sitting position. "You alright?"

"Yup."

A short time later, Taylor was lying on a jail cell cot with an ice pack on his head.

CHAPTER FIFTEEN

THE MAN KNELT ON THE kitchen floor of the diner. He carefully opened the silver can of Sterno purchased that afternoon at the truck stop outside of Stony Creek. Pulling a book of matches from his jeans pocket, he struck one against the coarse surface on the cover and watched it come alive. He touched it to the pink jellied alcohol, nearly burning his fingers. *Tonight I'll have a little heat,* he thought. Montana nights were still very chilly, even for June.

He placed a small can of beans on top of the fire and within minutes, they were warm enough to eat. Sitting cross-legged on the floor, he reached into a paper bag and retrieved a plastic fork and spoon. Lifting the beans off the flame, he set them on a cardboard placemat that he had fashioned from an old box.

The glow from the Sterno cast eerie shadows throughout the pitch-black room. The large gas stove loomed like a bear about to attack. The man had a flashlight but didn't dare use it. He worried that someone driving by might notice.

Finishing his beans, he set the can aside and rolled out his sleeping bag. Crawling inside he hunkered down. The light tapping of the exhaust vent opening and closing in the wind lulled him to sleep. He didn't have to sleep here like a homeless person. His 18-wheeler, parked at the truck stop, was more than

Stony Creek Diner

comfortable and warm.

CHAPTER SIXTEEN

CHARLIE PARKER STEPPED DOWN from the cab of his truck. He was nervous as a long-tailed cat in a room full of rocking chairs. This wasn't his first date with Sadie Abbott, but it was the first time she had invited him to her home since her husband, Cutter, passed away.

Removing his Stetson, he put his fingers to his mouth and slicked back his thinning hair with a bit of spittle. Straightening his bolo tie and brushing off imaginary dust from his jeans, he felt for his belt buckle and reassured that his fly was zipped. Clearing his throat, he headed for Sadie's porch steps.

"Damn." he muttered. Slapping his hat against his leg, he went back to the truck and opened the door to retrieve a large bouquet of wildflowers he had picked for her that afternoon.

From the minute Sadie heard Charlie's truck pulling into her driveway, she stood behind the curtains in the living room window peeking at him. She smiled, thinking he seemed nervous, but so was she.

Her heart pounding in anticipation, she knew tonight could change the dynamic of their relationship, either for the better or not at all. She scooted away from the window when he stepped up onto the porch.

Charlie inspected the hand-turn doorbell on Sadie's door.

It looked like solid brass with some detailed fancy flowers and scrollwork on it. *Humph. Something she must have picked up on one of her antique scavenger hunts.* He turned the crank and heard a "ring-a-ling".

Sadie loved the sound of her newly acquired doorbell. "Be right there," she called.

She had wanted to look casual and not made up. The mid-length denim skirt accented her mature figure. The plain, white V-neck cotton blouse with three-quarter length sleeves showed a hint of her ample assets while being respectable. A small black hills gold necklace lay just below the curve in her neck.

She glanced in the mirror. She had braided her long chestnut hair into a single braid. It hung loosely over one of her shoulders. Usually, she didn't wear make-up, but tonight she added a little blush to her round cheeks.

Before answering the door, she smoothed the skirt and tugged at the wide, dark brown suede fringed belt at her waist. She grinned, pleased with her overall appearance.

Opening the door, she greeted Charlie. "Welcome to my home." She stood back and ushered him into the living room. "Let me take your hat."

Charlie passed the Stetson to Sadie and thrust the wildflowers into her other hand. He cleared his throat again. "I thought you might like these."

She sniffed the bouquet. "Oh, I do, Charlie. They're beautiful. Thank you."

"So are you," he said shyly.

"What did you say?"

"I said you're beautiful, too."

Surprised, Sadie blushed like a sixteen-year-old schoolgirl receiving a compliment from a boy she liked. This was the first time a man had ever called her beautiful. She turned her head away, not wanting him to see the tears that had sprung up in her eyes. She brushed them away with the back of her hand.

"Are you okay?" he asked, putting his hand on her shoulder.

She faced him and smiled. "I'm more than okay, Charlie. That was the nicest thing anyone has ever said to me." Taking him by the hand, she led him toward the kitchen. "Are you hungry?"

"Starving," he answered, grinning and rubbing his belly.

"Have a seat." She motioned toward the table which had been set for two.

With care, he pulled out a chair, making sure it didn't scratch her pine floors, and lowered himself down.

The aroma from the elk stew simmering on the stove made Charlie's mouth water. He spied a pan of biscuits sitting on the counter ready for baking. He'd heard that Sadie made the best buttermilk biscuits of any woman in Stony Creek.

Glancing around the large kitchen, he was surprised to see that it was barely functional with appliances many years old. Doris, his deceased wife, came to mind. What a contrast between the two women. Doris would have had a fit if her kitchen had looked like this. Not that she was one to do much cooking, but she had to have the most up-to-date appliances.

Charlie felt like he had stepped back in time and into his mother's kitchen. Sadie's big black stove looked like it had come from the 1930's. If the refrigerator had not had an electric coil on the top, he would have mistaken it for one of the old-fashioned iceboxes. *Surely, Cutter could have done better for Sadie than this.*

Sadie noticed the frown on Charlie's face. "What do you think of my kitchen?"

He looked at her, his mouth slightly open. This was a lose-lose question and he knew it. Not wanting to put his foot in it, he remained quiet. He hadn't lived seventy-nine years and learned nothing.

"Charlie, it's not as bad as it looks. When Cutter was alive, I had all modern appliances. You know how much I love vintage things so when I was shopping for the store I ran across a few old items that I just had to have."

She pointed to the stove. "This old stove is a classic and works like a charm. So does the refrigerator. I bought a black slate sink, too. When I can find someone to install it, I'll have it in my kitchen and the stainless steel sink taken out. Sometimes I think I was born in the wrong era."

Walking over to the counter she picked up the pan of biscuits and popped them into the oven. "Wait until you taste what this old stove can do to my buttermilks."

Charlie looked sheepishly at Sadie, embarrassed that she could read his mind with such ease. He hoped she couldn't read the rest of what was going on in his head or she'd boot him out the front door before he had a chance to eat.

Sadie ladled out two steaming hearty bowls full of the savory stew and set them on the table. Charlie leaned forward and sniffed the mouth-watering aroma of the elk, potatoes, carrots and onions. A few minutes later Sadie took the biscuits out of the oven. Baked to a golden brown, she placed them on a plate and set them on the table.

"What would you like to drink, Charlie?"

"A glass of cold milk would be fine if you have any," he answered. Imagining how good the meal would taste, he wished Sadie would hurry up and sit down so he could dig in.

As Sadie was about to sit down, Charlie stood and pulled out her chair.

"Why thank you," she said sweetly.

"My pleasure."

"Would you mind if we say grace before we eat?"

"Not at all. I usually say a prayer to myself."

She put her hand out to him and he took it. An electric shock surged through his body feeling her warm skin in the palm of his hand. She bowed her head and Charlie did the same.

"Dear Lord, thank you for this bounty we are about to receive. Thank you for your daily blessings and for good friends who make our days much lighter. Please keep our country safe and those we love healthy and happy. In Jesus name. Amen."

"Amen," Charlie echoed.

Charlie picked up his spoon and dipped it into the delicious meal before him. He sipped the contents and let out a low moan. "Oh my gravy, Sadie. This is the best tasting elk stew I've ever eaten. My heart will probably stop beating when I bite into those buttermilks."

Beaming from his compliments, Sadie thanked him.

Later, relaxing on the sofa with a cup of freshly brewed coffee, Charlie couldn't remember the last time he felt this content. His belly was full and beside him sat the prettiest woman this side of Bozeman.

"That was one delicious meal. I could get used to this. Good food and a wonderful woman. What more could a guy ask for?"

Sadie didn't respond and turned her head away from Charlie's gaze. What did that mean, she wondered. Was she ready for a relationship? She was enjoying her freedom, but she knew she had strong feelings for him.

"Sadie? Did I make you uncomfortable by saying that?"

"Not really," she replied. "You've just given me some things to think about. Do you want more coffee?"

"I don't think so. I have to be up early tomorrow. I'd probably better get going anyway." He stood up and took Sadie's hand to help her to her feet. Gently he pulled her to him, and she let him. Using his finger, he raised her chin making sure she looked at him, Her cheeks flushed with anticipation. Charlie's breath was a little unsteady as he cupped the sides of her face with his callused hands. Lowering his mouth to hers, he kissed her lightly on the lips, enjoying the feeling of her body next to his. He held her for a long moment and then gave her a quick hug. With reservations, he let her go. "I'd better get out of here." Grabbing his Stetson, he made a beeline for the door.

"Charlie, wait."

Turning, he looked at her hoping he had not overstepped his bounds.

"This was the best evening I've spent in years. I don't know where this is going or if it's going anywhere, but I'm willing to give it a try if you are."

"Sadie, girl, you've just made me the happiest man in Gallatin County. I'll see you tomorrow?"

"I'd like that."

Opening the door, they stepped out onto the porch. Sassy, Sadie's Border collie and her three puppies greeted them. Sassy was excited to show her babies off. The puppies ran back and forth trying to herd each other.

"They sure are a bunch, aren't they?" Sadie grinned at the pups' antics. "I'll need to find a home for a couple of them before long."

"Well, good night," Charlie said, stepping down off the porch. He wanted to kiss her again but figured he better not press his luck and scare her away. "Tomorrow then?"

Sadie smiled and nodded.

CHARLIE LET HIMSELF INTO his house, happier than he'd been in a very long time. Noticing the answering machine blinking he pushed the message button.

"Hey Gramps. I've some news for you. I hope it will make you happy. I've decided to stay in Stony Creek and see if I can make a go of that old diner."

"Well, I'll be danged." Charlie reached up toward the heavens and shouted out a loud, "Thank you, Lord, for this wonderful day."

CHAPTER SEVENTEEN

MEREDITH AWOKE TO THE SOUND of whining and scratching at her front door. "What on earth is that?" She sat up and scratched her head, looking confused. Exhausted from a sleepless night of worrying about her decision, she grabbed her robe from the foot of the bed, wrapped it around her shoulders and made her way downstairs.

Cautiously, she peeked out the window. She saw a blur of fur running across her porch. Concerned that it might be a rabid animal, she reached for the shotgun in the corner. Inching the door open, she peered out. The animal took advantage of the opening and wiggled into Meredith's living room.

Heart beating wildly, she wheeled around ready to shoot. The fuzzy ball came running toward her and let out an excited yip. Her gaze widened. It was a Border collie pup with a note attached to its collar.

She bent down to remove the note from the black and white puppy, noticing that he was a boy. He reminded her of the Border collie she had when she was growing up. Pepper had followed her everywhere she went.

Since you've decided to stay in Stony Creek and make an old man happy, I figured you'd need someone to take care of. This little guy will be your constant companion and take good

*care of you, as he gets older. He doesn't have a name. That's
your job. Love, Gramps.*

Meredith reached down and patted the pup's coarse fur.
Just what I don't need, she mused, as he scampered off into the
next room.

"Hey, wait a minute," she yelled. The little dickens was
piddling in the middle of the kitchen floor.

She ran to pick him up, grabbing a paper towel to wipe up
after him. Once in her arms, he turned and licked her face while
scrambling to be put down.

"Oh no you don't." She held on to the wiggling mass of
fur. "You are going to learn to do your business outside and not
in the house."

She frowned. "Thanks a lot, Gramps."

She opened the kitchen door. Stomping barefoot down
the back steps, she plopped him onto the grass which was still
wet from the morning dew.

"Oh yuck," she groaned, lifting one foot, then the other.
The misty grass slid between her toes.

The pup squatted several times, not old enough yet to lift
his leg. Meredith smiled watching him sniff and mark the entire
yard making this new territory his own.

"Come on, boy," she called, slapping the side of her leg
to get his attention. Hearing her voice, the puppy bounded
toward her and up the porch steps.

On their way inside, she noticed that Gramps had left a
large bag of dog food, bowls, and a crate on the porch.

Meredith wiped the little collie off with a towel, but not
before he left a trail of footprints across the kitchen floor. She
set a bowl of water down for him which he sniffed and walked
in before he began to drink.

She desperately needed her morning coffee. What a crazy
way to start the busy day that lay ahead of her.

Walking toward the cupboard to get a coffee mug, the pup nudged up against her legs, almost tripping her.

"Hey there, mister, I'm doing just fine without your help."

She grabbed a cup and poured some of the hot liquid into it. Taking the first sip, she leaned back against the counter. Glancing at the kitchen clock, she grimaced.

"Oh no, it's seven thirty. Dakota is supposed to be here at eight and I'm not even dressed."

Carrying her cup with her, she started up the stairs to her bedroom. The little collie, right beside her, nudged her again and again, trying to herd her in another direction. Nearly losing her footing, the hot coffee sloshed out of the cup and spilled onto her bare feet.

"This has got to stop." Frustrated, she pushed him out of her way. Reaching the second floor with the pup still on her heels, she sat the coffee cup on a small table. Grabbing him by the scruff of his neck, much like his mother would have done, she gave him a gentle shake. In a stern voice, she said "No!"

He lay down on his belly, giving her a forlorn look, not understanding what he had done wrong.

Meredith moved toward the bedroom and again he was at her side, still prodding and herding. With her voice stern, she repeated the instructions once more, causing him to lie down after she scolded him. She knew if she was consistent it wouldn't take him long to learn since Border Collies are some of the smartest dogs on the planet.

After she was dressed, she and the pup headed downstairs. "I know what I'm going to name you." She smiled and gently petted her new companion. "Tripp seems like the perfect name, since that's what you've been doing to me ever since we met."

Tripp sat up and wagged his tail, looking at Meredith with what she could swear was a smile.

A quick rap on the door announced Dakota's arrival. "What do we have here?" he asked, spotting the small bundle of fur bounding from the kitchen.

"This is Tripp, thanks to Gramps. Seems he thinks I need someone to take care of. Personally, I think his timing sucks. Like I have nothing else to do."

"Why Tripp?"

"Poor little guy has been trying to herd me out to pasture. I nearly broke my neck going upstairs."

"He'll do his best to please you and he'll thrive on praise." Dakota paused and added, "On the other hand, you'll need to be the pack leader or he'll take over. It won't be pretty."

"I know. I remember when Pepper was small. Gramps was very stern with him and I used to think he was being mean. Now I know better. Pepper was the most loyal and smartest animal I ever had."

"Well, you haven't met Jake yet."

"Jake?"

"My German Shepard. He's out in the truck. I've left him home the past couple of times I've been over, but normally he's with me all the time. He'll be a great teacher for Tripp."

"We'd better get going," Meredith said, glancing again at the clock. "I'll go get the crate for Tripp. I'm not about to leave him loose in the house."

"Why don't we take him with us? Jake will take care of him. You need to socialize him early, Meredith, or he won't be worth much at all."

"Okay, if you say so."

Dakota and Meredith started for the front door, Tripp herding her all the way.

"No, Tripp," her stern voice made him stop nudging her. "He can't help himself," she laughed.

When they got to the truck, Dakota picked up Tripp and put him in the back with Jake. The large black and tan animal stood up, looming over the small puppy. Tripp put his tail between his legs and tried to sit down while Jake attempted to sniff his behind.

"That's just a dog's way of saying hello," he told Meredith. "Be good, Jake," Dakota warned. "Lie down." Jake obeyed while Dakota leashed Tripp's collar to the inside of the rear panel, making sure he couldn't fall or jump out of the back when the truck was in motion.

"You ready, Meredith?" he asked.

"Are you sure he'll be okay back there?" She was concerned. "Your dog didn't seem too happy to share his space."

"He was just checking things out. They'll be fine. Trust me. If you're ready, let's get going."

She nodded and walked around to the passenger's side of the truck. Dakota scooted past her and opened the door. "Why thank you, sir," she smiled broadly. *Chivalry isn't dead after all.*

Dakota grinned, closed the door and ran around to the other side of the vehicle.

Hopping up into the cab, he looked at her. "Let's go check out the diner."

He put the truck in gear, beaming from ear to ear. He was happy to spend the morning with the only girl he'd ever loved.

CHAPTER EIGHTEEN

THE MAN SUDDENLY AWOKE by the sound of dry, sharp gravel crackling under the tires of a vehicle pulling into the driveway of the diner.

Jumping to his feet, he peered through the small diamond-shaped window in the swinging kitchen door. Cold fear dampened his brow.

Sweet Jesus, I'm gonna' get caught this time.

It was the game warden and *her*.

He backed away from the door, grabbed his jacket from atop his sleeping bag and slipped out through the back entrance. A wrinkled piece of paper fell unnoticed from his jacket pocket and drifted to the floor.

The man couldn't risk going down to the highway. Someone would spot him for sure. The minute he stepped outside, that damned German shepherd in the game warden's truck started kicking up a ruckus.

In sheer panic, he ran up a small hill and through a wall of bushes, some with thorns hitting him in the face. He pushed them aside, not feeling the pain or blood that was oozing down his face. Running like the boogieman was after him, he eventually came to an old dirt path that led to the truck stop. Hearing no one following him, he stopped. He bent forward, bracing his hands on his knees and sucked in deep breaths of air before going on.

I can't keep doing this or I'm gonna' get myself killed.

He felt desperately lonely and weary to the bone.

A half-hour later, he arrived at the truck stop.

"Hey man, what happened to you?" another trucker asked.

"What do you mean?"

"You got blood dripping down the side of your face. Get in a fight or something?"

The man put his hand up to his cheek and felt the wet, sticky blood on his fingers. He pulled a handkerchief out of his back pocket and dabbed his face.

"Nothing like that. I was taking a walk in the woods and a couple of bushes whacked me in the face. Thanks for letting me know."

"No problem."

The man walked to his rig, pulled himself up into the cab, and closed the door. Lying down on his bed, he covered his face with his arms for a while. He needed a nap.

Waking after a fitful sleep, he turned on his side and reached for his jacket. He fished around in the pocket for the one thing that had held him together over the years.

"Holy shit," he grumbled, sitting straight up. It was empty.

"Where the....?" He rustled through the other pocket which held only a pack of gum. He clicked on the overhead light and turned the jacket inside out.

Where the hell can it be? Did it fall out in the diner? Oh God, I hope not.

Hands shaking, his head began to throb. What was he going to do?

"WHAT'S THE MATTER WITH THE DOGS?" Meredith asked Dakota, turning around to look out the back window. "They're sure spooked about something."

Jake, ears and tail erect with hackles raised, was running back and forth in the bed of the truck, barking frantically. Tripp, excited by Jake's behavior, was mimicking the big dog, barking in his high-pitched puppy voice and moving as much as his chain would allow.

"They're warning us about something," Dakota responded, opening the door and jumping down out of the cab. "You stay here. I'm going to take a look around."

Dakota went to the back of the truck and opened the tailgate. Jake bounded out. Tripp, still tethered, struggled at the chain.

Nose to the ground, Jake headed for the back of the diner. He stopped when he came to the rear open door, waiting for instructions from his master. Dakota leaned down and clasped a leash to Jake's collar.

He used the toe of his boot to fully open the door. Flashlight in hand he shone it about the room. Seeing nothing, he touched the dog on his back. "Go search," he ordered.

Jake stepped into the kitchen, straining at the leash, sniffing every corner.

They went towards the swinging door. A sleeping bag, opened cans and bottles were lying helter-skelter on the floor.

"The squatter's been here again," Dakota said to himself.

Hearing a sound in the diner, Jake let out a low growl and Dakota drew his weapon. Dog in front of his master, Dakota kicked the door open. "Hold it right there!"

"Good God, Dakota, put that gun away. It's just me," Meredith said, hands above her head.

"I thought I told you to stay put," he yelled. "How did you know someone wasn't hiding in here?"

97

"I figured they ran off when we pulled up and that's why Jake was acting up so."

"That's a good way to get killed, lady," he spat. "I know you have brains, but it doesn't look like you have much common sense." He pushed his hat to the back of his head and gave her a disgusted look.

"Are we fighting?" Meredith asked, an amused look on her face.

"I'm just trying to keep you alive, that's all. And wipe that smirk off your face. This isn't funny."

"I'm not as fragile as you may think, Dakota. I can pretty much handle myself these days, but thank you for wanting to take care of me," she said sweetly.

"Are you being sarcastic?" He frowned in obvious disapproval.

"Me?" she asked, leaning against the counter, eyes wide and innocent.

He snorted and turned away. *Damn, she makes me madder than a wet hen.*

Meredith walked over to Dakota. Playfully she poked him in the ribs. "So, what did you find?"

Her touch sent shock waves down his spine.

The moment was broken by Tripp's mournful howls, alone and still chained in the truck.

"Oh gosh, the pup." She turned away from Dakota and moved toward the diner door.

"Stay here, if you *can*," he said caustically, moving past her and out the door.

He retrieved the happy little collie who thanked him with juicy kisses. Setting him down in the grass to do his business, Dakota looked around. Seeing no one, he picked up the pup and went back into the diner.

Face still wet with puppy slobber, Dakota turned his attention to Meredith.

"What?" She cocked her eyebrows in question.

Dakota raised his arms over his head, a boyish grin on his face and strode slowly toward Meredith like a bear after his prey.

She pointed her finger at him. "You get away from me," she squealed, backing up and tripping over Tripp.

Dakota grabbed her, locking his arms about her waist. He rubbed his face over hers. Most of the puppy slobber had dried, but it was the idea of it that freaked Meredith out. "Yuk." She pretended to struggle for a split second, but then gave in to the electric tension between them.

She felt her cheeks flush as he looked longingly into her eyes. Slowly he settled his mouth over hers and she responded with a greed that left her weak.

She could feel him getting excited as his hand traveled to her breast. She groaned before covering his hand with her own. Breathless, she buried her face in his neck. "Dakota, we can't do this now. Please, stop." She wanted him in the worst way, but not like this, not here in the diner, not until she was sure where they were going. When they made love she wanted it to be perfect, not just a quick lay to release tensions.

"I'm sorry," he said, releasing her, his voice husky with emotion. "But you bring out the beast in me."

"I want this as much as you do," she responded. "It's not your fault. I just think it's too soon."

"Okay. I respect that. It'll be your call next time," he replied, sounding mildly rejected.

"I think we need to get to the business at hand," Meredith said, turning away from him. She pulled a small, green notebook and pen out of her purse. "I forgot a tape measure. Do you have one?"

Glad for the excuse to go outside and cool off, Dakota headed for his truck and toolbox.

Meredith looked the diner over extensively scribbling down all the work that would need to be done before she would be able to open for business. She left the kitchen for last, walking into the darkened room. *First thing I'm going to do is get electricity in this place.*

Dakota came in through the back door with a flashlight. "The squatter has been here again. He left a mess this time. You'd think that someone in town would notice a stranger hanging around."

She nodded. "The least he could do is clean up after himself. How is he getting in here?"

"Looks like he broke the old lock, but for some reason replaced it with a new one. Guess he's been using a key."

She took the light from Dakota noting the sleeping bag, cans of opened food, empty bottles of water, and a flannel shirt.

"What's this?" She leaned down and picked up the crumpled piece of paper. Shining the light on it, she gasped. Hands trembling she passed it to Dakota. "Oh my God, look at this!"

CHAPTER NINETEEN

JULY BURST FORTH WITH a flurry of activity and temperatures hot enough to fry an egg on a sidewalk.

Stony Creek was gearing up for its Fourth of July parade and annual picnic.

Meredith was busy looking for workers to repair the diner. With the decision made to stay, she couldn't wait to get started. She planned to have it operational by early fall, just before hunting season. It would take some sweat and hard work, but it could be done, *if* she could just find the help she needed.

The Fourth of July celebration is one of happy anticipation felt by the locals and those from nearby towns. Mayor Jasper and his committee had been busy for months preparing for the big event. Each year they strived to make the day bigger and better than the year before.

The agenda included the parade with the Black Mountain Senior Equestrian Drill Team performing, merchant street sale, 4-H exhibitions, a picnic at the State Park and a bake sale with proceeds going towards next year's event.

They planned a greased pig contest for the children, as well as a three-legged race in a potato sack, kick ball, Simon Says and Red Rover.

Softball and tag football were scheduled for the men, while the ladies gossiped and set up for the picnic. Maybe it wasn't fair, but it's the way it had always been and no one seemed to mind. The final event of the day would be a huge display of fireworks at the park.

MEREDITH ENTERED THE GENERAL STORE. "Hey Sadie," she called out. "Have you seen Gramps today? I can't find him anywhere."

Sadie came out from behind the hardware counter where she had been weighing and bagging nails for one of her customers.

"Meredith. It's so good to see you." She gave her a quick hug. "So, did your grandfather ask you to ride in the parade?"

"He did, but I told him no. Maybe next year. I haven't been on a horse in a long time and a parade isn't the place to get back in the saddle."

"What's that you've got under your arm?" Sadie asked, noticing the white placards Meredith was toting.

"Oh, these are some 'Help Wanted' posters," she replied, taking them from beneath her armpit. "If I want to get the diner fixed up I'm going to need to hire some help. Would you mind if I put one of these in your store window?" She showed the poster to Sadie.

HELP WANTED
LABORERS
SEE MEREDITH BANNING,
JULY 5TH, 8-11AM
AT THE OLD DINER ON RT 287

"Not at all, honey. I'll make a call to some of the guys who fixed up the vintage shop for me, and I'll pass the word along to my customers, too."

102

"Thanks, Sadie. I'm going to need carpenters, cleaners, anyone that can do just about any type of labor. Eventually I'll need a cook, other than myself of course, and a couple of waitresses."

"I'm so happy that you're staying. You're granddad is, too."

The jangling of the bell over the door announced a customer. Storm Anderson, all six and a half feet of him, strode into the store.

"Gage will be right with you, Storm," Sadie said.
The preacher acknowledged her with a smile. He tipped his hat toward Meredith. "Nice to see you again."

"Thanks. You, too."

"He's still single and the most eligible bachelor around, except of course for Dakota, Sadie whispered.

"He sure is good looking," Meredith murmured. She might care for Dakota but she wasn't dead, and the reverend was one hunk of man.

Sadie locked arms with Meredith and they walked outside. She began to snicker. Sitting in the front seat of Meredith's Mercedes convertible was the little Border collie that she had given Charlie; he was happily chewing on Meredith's Armani sunglasses.

"What have we got here?" she asked, pointing at the puppy with an amused look on her face.

Meredith shrieked. "Oh my God!" She bounded down the sidewalk steps, leaned into the car, and attempted to yank the slimy, mangled shades out of the pup's mouth. "Gimme'those," she yelled.

Ignoring her outburst, the pup gripped the glasses more firmly, wrapped both paws tightly around his possession and hung on for dear life.

"TRIPP! LET! GO!"

Tripp stood, locking eyes with his owner, head down, ears back, tail wagging furiously. Meredith was on one end of the ill-begotten sunglasses and the little dog on the other. Shaking his head back and forth, leaning low with his butt in the air, he let out a playful puppy growl. Tug of war was his favorite game.

"Fine, eat the damn things, see if I care," Meredith said in disgust, letting go of the glasses and placing both hands on her hips. "If they wreck your intestines, don't think I'm taking you to the vet, because I'm not," she wagged her finger at him.

Tripp sat down, sunglasses hanging out of the side of his mouth. He cocked his head from side to side, as Meredith walked away from the game as if to say, "Are we done playing?"

Sadie, doubled over in laughter, had a difficult time catching her breath. "Now that's a good one for the television show America's Funniest Home Videos."

"I'm glad you think it's so funny," Meredith retorted, wiping the puppy slobber off her shirt and arm.

Sadie stepped down off the sidewalk and stroked the pup's head. "So you named him Tripp? How'd you come up with that name?"

"Because tripping me is what he does best, other than eating hundred dollar sunglasses."

Sadie walked around the Mercedes. "Don't you think it's time you bought new transportation if you're going to stay here? You're lucky he didn't eat your leather seats. A truck would be more suited than this expensive car, don't you agree?"

"Look, I just made up my mind to stay a few days ago," Meredith answered in exasperation. "In the blink of an eye I have a four-legged herder to take care of, a diner to renovate, and you want me to get a new vehicle. Way too much for me to handle in such a short time."

Sadie's eyes twinkled. "Oh, I think you'll be able to handle everything just fine." She patted Meredith on the shoulder. "Your granddad's over at the café having breakfast. Why don't you go join him? I'll keep Tripp here with me while you're gone."

"Gladly," she said, scowling at her dog who was in the process of chewing on his leash, sunglasses abused and forgotten on the front seat.

She opened the car door, yanked the soggy leash from between the puppy's teeth, and handed it to Sadie. Tripp, happy to be free from his confinement, jumped out and licked Meredith's hand.

"You can say you're sorry all you want to, but I'm *still* pissed that you ate my glasses." Meredith absently gave the little dog a pat on his head.

"You go on now. Have a nice chat with your granddad. We'll be fine here." Sadie turned toward the store with Tripp, his mouth wrapped around the leash, trying to herd the way.

Meredith watched and shook her head before starting down the street. She stopped by Holbrook's Pharmacy, The Smokin' Barrel Saloon, and the banks to leave more posters. Arriving at the Powder Horn Café, the aroma of freshly brewed coffee beckoned her inside.

"Hey honey, over here." She looked across the room to see Gramps waving to her. Sitting next to him was Dakota, looking so fine she got all tingly inside. She walked toward the two men. Dakota flashed a welcoming smile and stood to pull a chair out for her.

"Thanks," she said, plopping down heavily. "What a morning this has been. Gramps, do you think you could drive to

Bozeman with me to pick out a truck? I think I'm going to trade Mercedes.

Dakota kicked Charlie's leg. "Ah, when do you plan on doing this darlin'?"

"I thought maybe tomorrow if you're not busy."

"Ah, sorry, can't do it tomorrow. I have other plans." He glanced in Dakota's direction.

"Doing what?" She eyed the two men. Gramps was lying through his teeth and she knew it.

"I'm not busy tomorrow so I can take you if you want," Dakota told her, his mouth twitching with laughter.

"You don't lie very well, Gramps. Is this a conspiracy? If it is, you two can just knock it off."

"I'd love to drive you to Bozeman tomorrow, really. Give a guy a break. I just want to spend some time with you."

"Well, okay then." She was too tired to argue and she did need to get a truck. Her belly quivered when she thought about spending the day with Dakota. "Come by around nine."

"I'll be there." He almost groaned aloud when visions of making love to her flittered through his mind. His thoughts must have shown on his face.

"Down boy," Charlie told him. "That's my granddaughter you're lusting after."

THE MAN SAT ON A BENCH at the end of the sidewalk watching Meredith as she went from store to store. When she entered the café, he walked over to the pharmacy to read the poster she had placed in the window. He rubbed his hand over his unshaven chin. "I never thought she'd come back to stay. Now what am I going to do?"

"Excuse me. Were you talking to me?"

He turned and looked straight into Sheriff Logan's eyes. His heart banged in his chest and his mouth went dry.

He swallowed past the lump in his throat. "Ah, nope. I was just reading this help wanted poster."

"If you're looking for a job, there's going to be plenty of work soon."

"Thanks, but I already have a job." He lowered the visor of his baseball cap and turned his head away.

"Well, in case you know of anyone out of work, tell them to go see Miss Banning at the old diner."

The man walked slowly down the sidewalk, willing himself not to run.

CHAPTER TWENTY

THE THERMOMETERS WERE READING 96° on the morning of the Fourth of July in Stony Creek. By 8 am, the sidewalks of Main Street were lined with vacant multi-colored webbed folding chairs,children sitting on the ground in front of them claiming their parent's *spot* for the 10 o'clock parade.

Doug and Dave Webster, the doc's twin sons, were dressed in matching cowboy outfits. They were riding their bikes up and down the street. Two friendly dogs ran along beside them, barking noisily and nipping at the wheels.

All the merchants were open for business. Store doors were held ajar by tables with items marked down to 50% off to entice people walking by.

Gage Boone carried four wooden rocking chairs out of the general store, two white, one red, and one blue and placed them on the sidewalk. He fastened a *reserved* sign on each of them for Sadie and her friends.

Sadie poked her head out of the door, looked around and smiled. She could feel the excitement mounting, even at this early hour. Hearing a faint rumble of thunder in the distance, she hoped it wouldn't rain and put a damper on the day's activities.

"Thanks, Gage," she said, as he set the last rocker down. Hearing a little child's laughter, she looked next door to the Vintage Shop. A tow-headed tot was having the time of his life riding the brown and white mechanical horse that looked like

Gene Autry's Champ. His mother was holding onto him so he wouldn't fall off.

On a recent shopping trip, Sadie purchased a bright red mechanical pig with white tusks, a black saddle and a curly tail. However, *Champ* seemed to be the children's favorite. She guessed most children in Montana would rather ride a horse than a pig.

"Gage, would you please bring the old green metal wash bucket outside? Fill it with ice, soda pop, and bottles of water. In this heat, people are bound to be thirsty." She wiped her brow with a hankie.

"Sure, Miss Cutter."

Before long there will be wall-to-wall people jamming the sidewalks and the street, she thought.

The Powder Horn Café was bustling with breakfast patrons and Jigger Johnson's Smokin' Barrel Saloon, had its share of morning imbibers.

When Gage brought out the wash bucket, he noticed his father going into the saloon. His gut wrenched for a minute. He worried that his dad would get drunk and cause a scene in front of the whole town. He went back inside to call his mother to warn her.

Sheriff Logan blocked off one end of the street to keep cars and trucks away from the parade area. He stationed a deputy at each end of the road for traffic and crowd control. The Sheriff and another deputy walked the sidewalks in case there was trouble.

A clown with colorful helium-filled balloons fastened with long strings worked his way through the crowd. He hushed a crying youngster by letting him honk his red bulbous nose and gave him one of the bright, yellow inflated toys. The little boy rewarded him with a big, toothless grin.

At 9:50 am, the first church bell chimed, alerting everyone that in ten minutes the parade would begin.

Men, women and children hurried out of the stores and found the spots they had reserved earlier. Others sat on the curb or stood. Fathers hoisted their small children onto their shoulders and mothers gave them little American flags to wave as the parade went by.

Sadie came out of her store and took a seat in the bright red rocking chair. Next to her were her three favorite friends, Willa Mae Johnson, Abigail Logan, and Anna Morgan. They chatted while they rocked in unison. Meredith, with Tripp lying at her feet, stood behind Sadie. She was excited as the children. This was the first parade she'd attended in many years.

At 10 o'clock, all five Stony Creek church bells sounded simultaneously, announcing that it was parade time.

The first strains of the high school marching band were heard in the distance. Heads turned to the left; little children, barely able to contain themselves, jumped up and down and pointed down the street.

A lone rider on a brown and white pinto, standing in his stirrups and holding the American flag, rode swiftly up the street in front of the people. A roar of appreciation went up from the crowd. He turned and galloped back down to where the rest of the participants were waiting for him.

He led the parade back up Main Street followed by six members of the Stony Creek Volunteer Fire Department carrying the Montana State Flag.

Closely behind was an outfitter leading his five mules laden with supplies over their backs. The mule in the rear was braying and kicking up his heels in protest, much to the delight of the children.

A large red, white and blue float pulled by a tractor slowly rolled by. Sitting atop in blue folding chairs was the local bluegrass band pickin' their banjos and making foot-stomping music.

Dakota, in the saddle on his beautiful buckskin horse, made Meredith inhale deeply. He was striking in his green game warden uniform. His dark black hair hung straight with a beaded band adorned with an eagle feather around his forehead.Spotting her with Sadie, he twisted in the saddle and flashed a grin.

Meredith hadn't expected his smile and she got all flustered. Embarrassed by her emotions, she quickly turned away, lost her balance and stepped directly onto Tripp's paw. He let out a loud yelp, jumped up, scrambled between Meredith's legs, and nearly upended her. Sympathizing with her puppy, Meredith looked over at Dakota who was laughing aloud as he continued down the street. *Damn him*! Sadie, Anna, Abigail and Willa Mae burst out laughing, too.

"Oh for God's sake," Meredith snapped, giving them the evil eye.

Behind Dakota was The Black Mountain Senior Equestrian Drill Team, all male riders in their 50's to 70 something working in unison to create a "dance" on horseback. The team consisted of eight members on black geldings decked out with white reins, halter, breast collar, and white wraps around the bottom of their legs.

Charlie was the lead, looking handsome in his black jeans and brocade vest, white shirt, white hat and black bow tie.

They stopped before the crowd and went through a short routine involving a series of patterns and maneuvers choreographed to music. Today's music was "Save a Horse, Ride a Cowboy" which made the crowd cheer and yell.

Sadie was beaming and realized at that moment she was deeply in love with Charlie Parker.

111

A float carrying veterans from World War I and II, the Korean War, Vietnam and the young men who had recently come home from Afghanistan and Iraq made up the remainder of the parade. Everyone stood when they rolled by, hands over their hearts, some saluting and many waving signs that said "Thank You."

When the last float rolled by, the crowd promptly dispersed. The events at the park would commence one hour after the parade was over.

TAYLOR BOONE STAGGERED OUT of the saloon, nearly falling off the sidewalk. His two friends, Ernie and Jackson, grabbed him. Holding him up between them, Taylor's arms hung over their shoulders.

"Let's get you home, pal," Ernie said, casting a sidelong glance at Jackson. Knowing Taylor, this wasn't going to be easy.

"I ain't going home," Taylor slurred. "I want to see my wife. She must be around here somewhere."

"Don't forget about the order of protection she put on you," Jackson reminded him.

"Screw the order of whatever it is. That don't scare me none. Hold on a minute. I gotta' take a piss."

The two men led Taylor into an alley. He leaned against one of the buildings to hold himself up while Ernie and Jackson kept a lookout for the sheriff or anyone else who might walk by.

Taylor finished his business, zipped himself up and smoothed down his shirt. "Let's go to the parade."

"The parade's all over, man. You slept through it in the Smokin' Barrel."

You gotta' be shittin' me," Taylor said, thrusting his thumbs in his jeans pockets and teetering back and forth on the heels of his boots.

"You guys know where I left my bike?"

"You're not going to be riding any motorcycle today," Ernie said. "I'm going to give you a ride home so you can sleep it off."

"I ain't ready to go home. Where's my damn bike?" Taylor shoved Ernie out of the way and started up the street. "My kid works in the General Store. He'll know where his ma is. Probably know where my bike is, too."

"Hey Taylor, come on, man. Let me take you home. You're not in any condition to go anywhere." Ernie took Taylor by the arm and tried to steer him in another direction.

Taylor took a swing at Ernie just as Sheriff Logan and one of his deputies came walking down the street.

"That's about all we'll have of that," the sheriff said gruffly, grabbing hold of one of Taylor's arms and twisting it behind his back.

"You son of a bitch," Taylor yelled and spit at him. Struggling to break away, jerking back and forth, he drew back his fist to hit the lawman. At that point, Sheriff Logan threw Taylor to the ground while maintaining his hold on him.

The deputy stepped in and the two men twisted Taylor's other arm behind him and cuffed him.

"Okay, mister, off to the pokey to sleep it off." They pulled Taylor to his feet and led him up the street to the jailhouse.

GAGE BOONE STOOD ON the sidewalk and witnessed his father's drunkenness and eventual arrest. He had called the sheriff to let him know his father was drunk and looking for trouble. Afraid for his mother, he made a vow never to let his father hurt her again. *One of these days, someone will kill him or he'll kill himself.*

CHAPTER TWENTY-ONE

MEREDITH WAS ON THE ROAD AT 7AM. The morning was bright with sunshine, but cool and crisp as she drove to the diner, windows ajar in her new truck, a bright red F-150, King Ranch edition.

The sights and sounds of the morning made her smile. She heard a meadowlark trilling his song and sitting on a telephone wire were two chatty magpies. Slowing down for a big yellow school bus, she noticed cattle in the field flapping at flies with their tails. Off the road and near the woods was a small herd of white tailed deer.

SHE THOUGHT BACK TO THE DAY BEFORE. The Fourth of July parade and festivities at the park had been wonderful. The best she could ever remember. The whole town had been in a joyous mood. The activities the mayor and his committee planned went off without a hitch.

Meredith met up with Dakota and his parents, Anna and Yuma, and spent most of the day and evening with them. Dakota and Yuma went off to play softball with the men while she and Anna walked through the park, stopping to chat with some of the locals. Meredith spotted a Fried Dough wagon. "I'll be right back, Anna. I haven't had fried dough since I was a kid, and my mouth is watering for some." She weaved her way through the crowd and stood in line until it was time for her to order. "I'll have mine with powdered sugar," she said excitedly to the young man who was taking orders.

Using tongs, he carefully lifted a hot piece of fried dough out of the boiling fat and placed it onto a paper plate, generously sprinkling powdered sugar over the top. "Be careful, it's hot," he told her as he handed it to Meredith along with several paper napkins.

"Thanks," she said as she paid him. She turned to go find Anna when she spotted a large aspen with no one claiming it. She hurried over and sat on the warm ground. She held the paper plate under her nose and inhaled the wondrous smell. Salivating, she pulled off a piece of the fried dough and slowly put it in her mouth. *Oh, I've died and gone to heaven. To hell with counting calories for today.* She spent a full half-hour eating her delicious treat before looking for Anna.

Anna had returned to their picnic table and was beginning to prepare for the evening meal. "There you are," Meredith said. "I looked for you and thought maybe you had come back here."

"How was the fried dough?" Anna asked. She smiled, noticing a spot of powdered sugar on the tip of Meredith's nose.

"It was de-licious," she drawled, licking her lips while she helped Anna cover the picnic table with a bright-checkered tablecloth and secure it with colorful plastic clips.

Anna retrieved fried chicken, sliced roast beef, ham and cheese sandwiches, coleslaw, and potato and macaroni salads from her picnic basket. From a cooler she brought out condiments, soft drinks, and beer. She pulled an assortment of paper plates, plastic cups and cutlery, and a roll of paper towels from a cloth grocery bag and placed them on the table. She seemed to do it effortlessly and with enjoyment.

She placed her hands on her hips and surveyed the table, looking for any items she may have forgotten. Shortly, Dakota and Yuma returned from their game and Gramps and Sadie joined them.

"Anna, would you consider being my chef at the diner when I open it?" Meredith asked her, munching on the best fried chicken she'd eaten in a long time.

"I don't think so," she replied, shaking her head, her long braid swinging back and forth behind her. "I have more than enough to keep me busy taking care of the ranch house, my own place, and your grandfather."

"It wouldn't be full time," Meredith responded,"because I'm going to be cooking there myself. I just need someone who knows how to cook the dishes that Montanans love so much like elk stew, buffalo burgers, and your delicious pan-fried trout."

"Go ahead, Anna," Gramps chimed in. "I can get along without you for a few hours a day or even a few days a week if you want. My house stays clean most of the time and Sadie, here," he smiled at Sadie and gave her a quick squeeze, "has been feeding me some wonderful meals lately." He patted his tummy. "As you can all see, I'm losing my girlish figure thanks to her cooking."

They all laughed.

Anna glanced over at Yuma. "Hey," he said, raising both hands up in front of him. "Don't get me involved in this so I end up being the bad guy. No matter what I say, it's a no win situation for me. You make your own decision."

"Well, I'll think about it, but don't count on it."

"That's all I ask," Meredith said.

After they were fully sated, they all chipped in with the cleanup, retiring to camp chairs set up around the picnic table.

As day turned to dusk, the festivities took on a party atmosphere. A local country band, Big Sky Brothers Band, was setting up on a stage that had been erected above the makeshift dance floor. Lights, strung around the area, came on as soon as it was dark.

The band, all tuned up, began with a slow song, *Could I Have This Dance.*

Dakota leisurely raised himself from his chair, sauntered over to Meredith with a wide grin on his face, and held his hand out to her. She smiled back and extended her hands to him. He pulled her to her feet and put a protective arm about her waist while they walked to the dance floor.

"I love this song," Meredith said as she wrapped her arms tightly around his neck and laid her head on his chest. She could feel his heart thudding beneath his shirt as they swayed back and forth to the music.

He kissed the top of her head and murmured something she couldn't quite make out. She leaned back and looked at him in question. He smiled and gently pushed her head back onto his chest, tightening his arms around her waist.

The music ended. Meredith was about to step away and break her hold from Dakota when the band started playing the Electric Slide. Half the town, including children, joined in. She was surprised to see Gramps and Sadie kicking up their heels and a big shock was seeing Reverend Anderson line dancing next to Carrie Boone. Carrie was having the time of her life, dancing and smiling as if she didn't have a care in the world. *I hope Taylor doesn't show up,* Meredith thought. *There'll be trouble for sure.*

For the remainder of the evening they line danced, square danced and slow danced the night away. During a break, Dakota whisked Meredith behind a large aspen and kissed her until her knees were limp as dishrags.

I am so falling in love with this man.

AS MEREDITH ROUNDED THE BEND in the road, the diner came into view. She was astonished to see about twenty or so people waiting for her in response to the ads she had placed around town. She pulled into the driveway, turned off her truck, and hopped out.

"Hey, everyone. So glad to see you all. I'll just be a minute getting the diner open and then we can go in."

Walking up the temporary steps to the front door, Meredith unlocked it with her rabbit's foot keychain. Once inside, she waved them in behind her.

"Take a seat everyone," she said, motioning them to the bar stools and booths. A few would have to stand.

"I'm so glad to see all of you. As you can see this old diner is in need of fixin-up. Fortunately, she has good bones. I feel that with some old-fashioned elbow grease we can have her looking almost new in no time."

Meredith scanned her notes before going on. "First things first. I need electricity. I've called the power company and they're going to bring a pole and get the power hooked into the diner the first of next week. Is anyone here an electrician?"

"Right here," a man sitting on one of the bar stools raised his hand. He stood and introduced himself, offering Meredith his hand. "I'm Will Stevens and own an electrical business. I put the wiring in for Sadie at her vintage shop." He passed her his business card. Stevens Electric, Licensed, Insured and Bonded. (406) 285-1212. Will Stevens, Proprietor.

"Thanks Will. Sounds great. See me later and I'll go over the details with you."

"Next, I need to have a wide driveway made, large enough to hold several cars and possibly one or two big rigs. The area will have to be cleared out, graded, and dirt hauled in. I may think about tarring a portion of the driveway if we can get it done before it gets too cold. Any takers for this job?"

Ernie Loomis raised his hand.

"Ernie?" she questioned.

"Hey, Meredith. I've had my own construction business for a few years now. I've got some good references so if you'll give me a chance I don't think you'll be disappointed."

She hesitated for a minute. "When I'm done talking to Will, we can talk, Ernie. I'd like to hear what you have to say."

"Thanks," he said, and sat back down.

Meredith spent the next hour explaining her ideas, wants and needs for the diner. Everyone was eager and available for immediate work. By the time her list was completed she had herself a crew of workers.

Carrie Boone surprised Meredith by asking to help clean. She also was applying for a waitress position once the diner opened. She was living with her parents and wanted to get out on her own with her boys. Meredith still didn't like her much, but she was willing to give her a chance to get back on her feet.

Ernie Loomis lagged behind after the others left. He waited for Meredith inside the diner while she was outside talking to Will. Looking around the diner, he knew that if anyone could make a go of this place it would be her.

The door opened and Meredith stepped inside. "So, Ernie, you want the job of making me a driveway and all that goes with it?" She sat down on one of the stools.

"Yes, I do."

Slowly swiveling around, she looked intently at Ernie. "Am I going to have to worry about you starting the job, drinking, and leaving me holding the bag?"

"Hell no, Meredith. I'm married now and have a couple of kids. Believe it or not, I don't drink." He shrugged his shoulders and shoved his hands in his pockets, obviously uncomfortable. "I know every time you've seen me it's been with Taylor, but he's the one with the drinking problem. He makes us guys look bad, but, he's been my friend all of my life. Most times when I'm with him it's because I feel sorry and want to make sure nothing happens to him."

"Does Jackson work for you?" she asked him.

"He does. He drinks a couple of beers now and then, but he's married, too. His wife would knock him over the head with a frying pan if he came home drunk. She's quite a feisty one."

Meredith chuckled at the thought.

"If I hire you for the job, you'll promise me that you'll come to work every day and get the job done on schedule?"

"That's what I'm telling you," he responded, nodding his head.

"Ok then, we'll give it a try. By the way, I don't want Taylor hanging around here. Is that understood?"

"Understood."

For the next hour they discussed Meredith's plans for the driveway, with Ernie suggesting a few changes here and there. When they finished, he told Meredith he'd be in touch in two days with his estimate, knowing in his mind that he was going to do the job for her. "Thanks Meredith. I won't let you down." Ernie let himself out of the diner.

CHAPTER TWENTY-TWO

BY THE FIRST OF AUGUST, POLES and power lines were in place. Will Stevens rewired the diner and increased the amperage by installing a new circuit breaker panel. After passing inspection, the power company installed a meter on the diner and ran the wires to it. It was a red-letter day when Meredith ceremoniously flipped the ON switch and the diner lit up. "Now we can really get to work," she said, grinning at Will.

Ernie Loomis, true to his word, had undertaken the job of constructing a large parking lot. Brush was cleared away, dirt hauled in and smoothed out, and with enough time, before cold weather set in, the driveway had been paved.

He also built a new wide entryway into the diner which would accommodate wheelchair use, adding railings on both sides for safety.

Carrie and several ladies from town, along with a few men, were hired to do the cleaning. Carrie was excited to start work and be independent of her parents. She hoped that soon she would be able to afford an apartment or place of her own for her three boys. She wanted to file for divorce, but that took money which she didn't have. Her parents would have gladly paid so she could be rid of Taylor, but Carrie wanted to do it on her own.

Meredith sat down outside, feeling the cool concrete of

the new steps beneath her and took in the quiet of the morning. She could hear the clackety-clack of a slow moving train in the distance. Everything was coming together just as she had hoped. Tomorrow, restorations would begin on the inside. It would be a big undertaking, but she had enough help for the project.

An 18-wheeler rolled on by. The driver pulled his air horn to say hello. Meredith waved. The man inside the cab smiled.

LATER THAT AFTERNOON, Meredith met with Anna to discuss the menu. Anna had agreed to be the interim cook, but only if it didn't interfere with her duties to Charlie. Heads together over a cup of hot coffee in Meredith's kitchen, they agreed and disagreed on what the locals would like.

"One thing I'm sure of is that we'll serve breakfast all day," Meredith said, curling one foot under her. "The men like a nice hot meal after hunting in the cold. I've been in touch with Wheat Montana and plan to buy my baking products from them."

"That *could* interfere with the Powder Horn's breakfast," Anna reminded her. "You don't want to get on the bad side of the merchants who've made a living here for years."

"You're right, I don't," she replied, her jaw flexing as she clenched her teeth. "However, the diner is further out of town and probably wouldn't get as many locals as much as the Powder Horn. And anyway, I think this town is big enough for more than one establishment that serves food. Our menus will be different so I really don't see a problem. I've spent a lot of money and time on this project, but at the same time I'm not going to deliberately step on anyone's toes."

Anna could tell from Meredith's demeanor that she was getting a little hot under the collar. "I just wanted to remind you of how tough it was when this town wasn't more than a dirt road with sagebrush tumbling through it," she said softly. "These men have worked through blood, sweat and tears to turn this town into what it is today."

"Stony Creek is a beautiful and prosperous little cowboy town," Meredith agreed, "and I'm honestly happy to be part of it again. I never thought I'd hear myself saying that, but it's true. I'll do my very best to make the diner work and stay in everyone's good graces at the same time."

"Let's get back to work then," Anna said, giving Meredith a pat on the hand.

A couple of hours later they had a menu prepared. Meredith would take it to Willow Creek print shop and have them make seventy-five laminated copies which should be enough to start with.

EARLY THE FOLLOWING MORNING, the clean-up crew, armed with buckets, mops, and cleaning supplies they picked up from the General Store per Meredith's request, arrived at the diner. Meredith made sure she got there before them. When they entered the diner, the Bunn coffee maker was gurgling and sending out the delicious aroma of freshly brewed coffee. Meredith laid out paper plates, cups, and muffins from Wheat Montana's bakery.

"Hi, everyone. Glad to see you. Are you ready to clean this place up and make it a sparkling diner?"

"Thanks so much for this opportunity," Carrie piped up.

"No thanks, necessary. Why don't we all have a cup of coffee and a muffin before we get busy? Everyone, please, sit down."

Grabbing a muffin and coffee, they took a seat, some in booths and others at the counter. Meredith mentally noted there were fifteen people, ten women and five men. She would have the men go outside to work, keeping the ladies inside with her.

"I'd like to go over exactly what I want done. The health inspectors will be here before I open and I want this place immaculate." She picked up a notebook from the counter. "The outside has been power washed, but it needs to be wiped down and the windows need to be washed inside and out. I'll have the men do those. Ladies, the rest is up to you. There is a lot of stainless steel in here and I want to be able to put my makeup on when I look into it." The ladies nodded their heads and smiled. "Okay, then. Let's get busy."

For the next several hours, the crew worked steadily. Meredith fed quarters into the little table jukeboxes to keep their spirits alive with country tunes. They cleaned, sang and wiggled their fannies to the music. When a slow song came on, Carrie grabbed a broom and danced her partner around the diner. Everyone laughed and clapped. Meredith had never seen this side of Carrie and she liked her sense of humor. The men, on their ladders, looked in the windows and shook their heads. One of them made a circular motion to his head suggesting they were all crazy.

By late afternoon, the front portion of the diner was spic and span. The stainless steel backsplash shone like a baby's bottom. The five-burner BUNN coffee maker was sparkling. The old Wyott creamer was shining and a missing nut in the portion adjustment had been replaced. The large two-door refrigerator-freezer was gleaming. Meredith could see her face in it. She grabbed her purse, took out her lipstick, and painted her lips a light bronze.

"Good job, ladies," she said, giving them a thumbs up. "How about we call it a day? You can come back tomorrow, same time, and we'll tackle the floors and the kitchen."

The loud roar of a motorcycle interrupted the chatter. Carrie turned ashen. She looked at the front door as she started for the rear.

"Carrie, wait," Meredith ordered. "Let me take care of this." She opened the door and walked out onto the steps. The men, still on ladders, kept a watchful eye.

"Where's my wife?" Taylor shouted. "I want her out here, now!"

"She's inside and she's not coming out as long as you're here," Meredith said. Her eyes narrowed and her face turned hard.

Taylor turned off his bike and put the kickstand down. The men climbed down the ladders, and stood waiting for the next move.

"Hey guys, you know me. I don't mean any harm," Taylor said, running his hand across his forehead. He was suffering a bitch of a hangover and just wanted Carrie to come out and go home with him. "I want to see Carrie. I..I need to get her back," he whined. In the next breath, he turned surly and mean. "She's being such a bitch though; won't answer my calls, won't let me see my boys or anything. I thought I'd come by, give her a ride home and maybe talk some sense into her."

"You'd better leave before I call the sheriff," Meredith said, feigning a cool indifference. She could feel in her bones that Taylor was about to snap if she didn't draw his mind away from Carrie. She was confident he didn't want to be arrested again, but just in case there was trouble, she opened her cell phone and started to dial 911.

"Well, fuck all of you then," he yelled. "Especially you, Meredith. You might look different now, but to me you'll always be the fat hog with four eyes and bushy hair." He started up his bike and sped off, leaving rubber on the newly paved driveway.

Meredith sucked in a deep breath and gulped back the emotions that were swelling up inside her. After all these years, Taylor Boone still had the means to hurt her feelings. The son of a bitch! Clenching both fists at her sides, she turned around and went back inside.

Carrie was sitting on a stool crying and the other women were trying to console her. "I'm so sorry, Meredith. I won't come back tomorrow. He's never going to let me go and I'm afraid one of these days, he'll kill me. I don't want anyone else to get hurt because of me."

Meredith took Carrie by the shoulders, gave her a small shake and looked at her. "You *will* come back tomorrow because I need you and you need to get a place for you and your boys. We're not about to let Taylor run our lives. You got that?"

Carrie wiped her nose and nodded. "Thanks. I'll be here in the morning."

"Good. You need to know, Carrie, that if he pulls into this driveway one more time I'm going to have him arrested on the spot. When I leave here, I'm going to stop at the sheriff's office and have an order of protection served on him. Are you okay with that?"

"I'm okay with it. I can't seem to stop him, but maybe someone else can."

"All right everyone, lets pack up and get out of here for today. I'll see you all tomorrow. Thanks guys for coming to the rescue."

The men smiled and tipped their hats. On the way out she heard one of them say, "She sure put Taylor in his place. I wouldn't want to tussle with her." They murmured in agreement.

CHAPTER TWENTY-THREE

TAYLOR BOONE WAS MADDER THAN HELL when he sped away from the diner. *Who did Meredith think she was anyway? She's gonna' be sorry she made a fool of me in front of all those people. And wait 'til I get my hands on Carrie. She'll be sorry she didn't come out and talk to me. She's gonna' get hers, big time. First, I need to make the other bitch pay for what she did, and the sooner the better. When I get done with her, she'll be making plans to head out of town...forever!*

He revved the throttle and kicked the motorcycle into high gear. Going too fast around a corner, the bike started to slide on some loose gravel. For a split second, his life flashed before him as he felt the bike skidding out of control. Somehow, he managed to compensate and stay upright. "Shit, shit, shit, that was too damned close!" His heart was beating faster than a trip hammer, his brow and hands were clammy. He slowed the bike while trying to get his nerves to calm down. Continuing into town, he pulled up in front of the Smokin' Barrel Saloon. What he needed was a stiff drink.

MEREDITH LOCKED UP THE DINER and headed into town. She had a bad feeling about Taylor so her first stop would be at Sheriff Logan's. As she drove by the saloon, she noticed Taylor's bike parked outside. He was in a foul mood when he left the diner and surer than anything he would be looking for trouble before the day ended.

Meredith pulled her truck up to the curb in front of the sheriff's office. She ran her hands through her hair to freshen up a bit before going inside. She took a deep breath, collected her thoughts and got out of the vehicle. She opened the door to the office. The sheriff was asleep at his desk and didn't hear her come in.

"Sheriff? Sheriff, Logan. You okay?"

His body jumped with a start, his feet dropped to the floor, and he looked at Meredith, a bit confused. He shook his head, stood and stretched. "Oh, hey Meredith. I must have dozed off for a minute. It's been a slow day."

"It may get a little busier for you before too long. Taylor Boone is at the Smokin' Barrel and madder than a wet hen at me."

"Why's that?"

"He came to the diner today and demanded to talk to Carrie. She was scared to death so I made her stay inside and I went out to confront him. He didn't take kindly to some woman telling him to get off her property."

"I don't imagine he did. Did he threaten you?"

"I'm probably the one who did the threatening. I told him if he didn't leave right then that I was going to call you and I'd have him arrested. He slung some four-letter words around but he left."

"So what can I do for you?" He dropped back into his chair and crossed his arms in front of his chest.

"How do I go about getting an order of protection against him?" she asked.

"Well, we can file here but it will still have to go before a judge who will decide whether or not to issue the order. It's all up to him, unfortunately."

"Do you know whether Carrie has an order in case he tries to hurt her again?"

"By law, I can't really say, but I will say that she's about as safe from him as she can be."

"I'm really more concerned for my employees. Although Taylor did back down when the five guys who were working for me climbed down off their ladders, all at the same time. He sang a different tune then."

"Most times Taylor's bark is worse than his bite, that is, unless you're a woman. He likes to beat them up. Do you want to file, Meredith?

"Maybe I'll hold off for a while and see what happens. If he comes back on my property or to the diner again, I will have him arrested for trespassing. I warned him today and I'm going to keep my word."

"Well, if he bothers you again give me a call and I'll take care of him."

"Thanks, Sheriff. I never wanted to come back to Stony Creek in the first place, but now that I'm here, I'm beginning to like it. Gramps is so happy I'm home that it makes it all worthwhile."

"Did I just hear you say you're home?" he asked cupping his ear at the word.

"Well, I guess you did. Maybe I am home after all."

"How about Dakota? I've seen a mighty big smile on your face when you look at him."

"He's a wonderful man and I'm really happy we can be friends again. It's been way too long. Well, I'm on my way home. Tripp has been visiting with Sadie and I have to stop by and pick him up."

"Give me a call if you need me."

"I will. Thanks again." She stepped outside just in time to see Taylor speeding down the road on his motorcycle. He saw her standing in front of the sheriff's office and gave her the finger.

The hair on the back of her neck tingled. She didn't know what was on his mind, but she knew he was up to something.

TAYLOR RACED DOWN THE FRONTAGE ROAD toward his in-law's home. He was still furious at Carrie for making a fool of him in front of some of the town's men who were working for that bitch, Meredith. Carrie didn't need to work anyway. All she needed to do was come home and mind her business.

He took a sharp right onto Madison, a narrow two-lane dirt road, bumping over the railroad tracks. He'd had a few too many at the saloon and was pushing the limit with how well he was able to ride. He needed to pay attention so he wouldn't end up dumping the bike like he nearly did a few hours ago.

He zigzagged back and forth over the washboard ruts, beginning to think that this might not be such a good idea after all. Larry and Linda lived four miles down the road. It was going to be a long, bumpy ride for him.

Carrie was outside hanging clothes when she heard the motorcycle in the distance. Her heart sprang into her throat and she began to panic. Running inside she grabbed the phone and called her mother who was at work.

"Ma, I can hear Taylor's bike coming down the road. What should I do?"

"Are you sure it's him? Lots of people have bikes, honey. Maybe it's your dad. He took his bike to work this morning."

"Oh, it probably is then. Whew! I was so scared."

"Stay inside, Carrie, until you know for sure, and whatever you do, if it is Taylor, don't let him in. Hurry and lock the doors. The minute you see him call the sheriff. I'm going to

Stony Creek Diner

call your dad and come right home."

CHAPTER TWENTY-FOUR

LINDA PUSHED BACK FROM HER DESK at the Methodist church where she volunteered twice a week helping Reverend Anderson with clerical duties. Worry lurked in her eyes. She grabbed her sweater and purse and strode toward the door. Hurrying down the hall to his private office, she called out. "Reverend Anderson?" No answer.

She called louder, "Reverend!"

Storm Anderson excused himself from his meeting with a parishioner to see what was wrong with his secretary. He could hear in her voice that it was something serious. Stepping out into the hallway he nearly collided with her.

"Whoa, hold on there, lady," he said, putting his hands on her shoulders. "What seems to be the matter?"

"I have to leave," she said breathlessly. "Carrie called and said she thinks Taylor is on his way to the ranch. She's alone and terrified. I have to go to her."

"By all means," he said, "but I don't think you should go alone. I'll tell Mrs. Wilbur I have an emergency. She'll understand."

"Please hurry. I don't know how much time we have. Dang," she said, shaking her head to rid her mind of the cobwebs floating in to confuse her.

"Sorry Reverend. I got so frazzled I haven't even called Larry or the sheriff yet." She pulled her cell phone out of her purse and hit speed dial for her husband.

The phone rang several times before prompting Linda to Larry's voice mail.

"Larry Owens."

"Larry. Call me the minute you get this message! I'm afraid Taylor is heading to the ranch to hurt Carrie. Reverend Anderson and I are on the way. Please come home if you can."

"Oh God, I should have called the sheriff first," she berated herself. "What *is* the matter with me?" She punched #9 on her speed dial as they were leaving the rectory.

"Sheriff's office." Deputy Tucker Murphy answered the phone.

"This is Linda Owens," she said brusquely. "Is Sheriff Logan there?"

"No, Miss Owens. He had to drive over to Willow Creek for a meeting."

"Please try to contact him," she said, gripping the phone, her voice shaky. "Tell him Taylor Boone is on his way to my ranch to have an altercation with my daughter, Carrie. Please hurry!"

"Yes, ma'am, I'll contact him right away," Deputy Murphy said, "and in the meantime I'll head on out to your place. Does Taylor usually carry a weapon?" he asked.

"I don't think so, but I can't say for sure," she answered.

TUCKER MURPHY, 21 YEARS OLD, was new to the Sheriff's department. He'd only been a deputy for a little over a year and hadn't seen much action except for passing out a few traffic tickets or breaking up a bar room brawl.

YEARS AGO, WHEN HE WAS JUST A YOUNGSTER, Tucker and his mother had taken a trip over to Billings. On the way home, the weather turned fierce and their car slid off the road. They waited for what seemed like hours, at least to a small boy it seemed like hours, the wind howling and the snow blowing around them.

Tucker's mother wrapped him up in an old blanket she kept in the car for such an emergency as this. She occupied him by playing "I see something blue" and then they would name everything that was blue in the car. Next, it was his turn to pick. Just about the time they ran out of colors and the cold was beginning to seep into their bones, they heard a knock on the window.

"Who's there?" Tucker's mother called out.

"Highway Patrol, ma'am."

"Thank God," Sarah Murphy said. She tried to roll down the window. It was frozen. She tried to open the door and it, too, wouldn't budge. Hearing a few hard raps on the outside of the door, it opened and a burst of fresh snow fell in on them.

The trooper's gloved hand was on top of the open door and he leaned down and peered inside at them with a huge smile on his face. He was their hero, their rescuer, Trooper Wayne Mitchell. What fascinated Tucker the most that day was Trooper Mitchell's Smokey Bear hat and bright shiny badge. Sarah, on the other hand, was fascinated with the most beautiful smile she had ever seen.

"Howdy, ma'am. Are you folks all right in there?" Sarah and Tucker nodded.

"I've got a tow truck on the way and we'll have you out of here in just a few minutes."

From that day on, Tucker knew he wanted to be a Highway Patrol Officer when he grew up.

Fate was not in his favor though. During his junior year in high school, a horse threw him and his leg was badly injured.

HE APPLIED FOR THE HIGHWAY PATROL ACADEMY after graduation, but didn't pass the agility test due to his old injury. He was disappointed, but not one to give up on a lifelong dream, he decided to become a deputy, hoping that someday he'd be someone else's hero or rescuer. *Today might just be the day*, he thought, while he sped out to the Owens' ranch.

TAYLOR WAS HAVING A DIFFICULT TIME keeping his bike on the road. He was totally drunk, royally pissed off and ready to knock some sense into Carrie. The more he thought about her, the madder he got, and the faster he tried to get to her.

His breathing was unsteady, eyes narrowed, nostrils flared and his mouth was set in a tight line, much like a bull ready to charge. He was full of pent up anger and frustration and today she would listen to him, dammit, or else.

From afar, he could make out the sound of a siren and he drove a little faster. *What a bitch! She called the sheriff and I ain't done nuthin' wrong.* He gritted his teeth. He knew he was in trouble. *I gotta' turn around and head back. I'm gonna' get arrested and land in jail again.* He slowed the bike to make the turn when he noticed the grader had been through and the road just ahead was smooth. *To hell with turning back.*

"Carrie!" he screamed her name at the top of his lungs.

He shifted into high gear, hands clutching the handlebars in a death grip. The siren behind him was louder and closer, and he drove faster and faster. *Only one more mile and I'll be there.*

Out of nowhere, a white-tailed buck jumped across the road in front of Taylor's speeding bike. There was no time for him to avoid the inevitable and he hit the deer broadside, ejecting him from the bike, over the handlebars and through the air.

Taylor Boone's last thought, just before his helmetless head collided with a large Ponderosa Pine, was *Oh, fuck!*

CHAPTER TWENTY-FIVE

"OH MY, GOD!" DEPUTY MURPHY SHOUTED, witnessing Taylor's body connecting with the tree. He slammed on the brakes, the cruiser skidding sideways to a stop on the gravel. He jumped out leaving the engine running and the door open, and rushed over to Taylor. One look and bile rose up in his throat. Tucker gagged and turned away, but couldn't control the vomit that spewed out of his mouth. This was his first fatality and it couldn't have been worse.

Tucker wiped his mouth on his sleeve and looked back at the body, wishing there was something he could do, but knowing at the same time it was futile. *I'm not going to touch him, even though I know I should to see if he's alive. I'm such a coward. I can't do it.*

Reverend Anderson and Linda showed up minutes later. "Stay right here," he told her. She had both hands clasped over her mouth. "You okay?" he asked. She shook her head, frozen in shock over what had just happened.

Storm pushed the car door open and stepped outside. He squared his shoulders and inhaled deeply, then walked over to where Tucker was standing.

"It's really bad, Reverend. You sure you want to look?"

"I have to," he answered. "Is he alive?"

"I don't know," Tucker replied.

137

Reverend Anderson squatted next to Taylor's body and felt for a pulse. There was none. "Have you called the volunteer rescue yet?" he asked Tucker.

"I haven't but, I'll...I'll do that right now." Tucker Murphy was failing miserably at his job. *The sheriff will probably fire me before the day is over,* he thought, grabbing the microphone and requesting rescue service from dispatch. "Oh, better get Doc Webster out here, too," he told the dispatcher.

Storm stood up and looked over toward his car. Linda was standing outside. He shook his head and she began to cry, putting her hand to her mouth.

Larry arrived, bringing his vehicle to a dead stop in the middle of the road. He'd swapped vehicles with one of his co-workers leaving his bike behind and using his friend's car. He knew from the sound of Linda's voice on her message that this was urgent and he wanted to get to her as fast as he could. Linda ran over to him and threw her arms around him the minute he emerged from the car.

"What the hell happened?" he asked his wife who was near hysteria.

Storm walked over to Larry. "Taylor was in a fatal accident with his motorcycle. Hit that big tree there with his head."

"Jesus! Was he alone?" Larry asked. He feared one of his grandsons was with him.

"He was alone. Looks like a deer jumped out in front of him and he hit it. He must have been going awfully fast from the look of things."

Larry gently removed Linda's arms from around his neck and walked over to where Taylor was lying, half wrapped around the base of the tree.

Larry cupped his chin with his hands feeling the stubble of his beard with his fingers. He looked at the broken body lying before him. Swallowing hard he shook his head. He wanted to feel something; sad, mad, compassion, anything, but all he felt was a sense of relief and gratitude that his daughter's life would no longer be in jeopardy.

He pushed his hat toward the back of his head and shoved his thumbs in his jeans pockets. He blew out a big breath of air. "Well, buddy," he said to the broken body lying before him, "I hate to say this, but what goes around, comes around." He turned and walked back to his wife.

Larry, Reverend Anderson and Tucker hauled the dead deer out of the road while waiting for the rescue. They left Taylor's body and his bike where they were. That job was up to the rescue team, Doc, and Sheriff Logan.

Residents of Madison Road, on their way home, came upon the grisly scene. Not being able to continue they stopped their vehicles and got out to look. It didn't take long for news to get out that Taylor Boone had met his maker.

The school bus carrying Dusty and Danny Boone made a U-turn in the middle of the road when the driver got word that Taylor was dead. It took him a few tries to turn the big bus around, taking the children away from the dreadful scene ahead. "Okay, kids. Get back in your seats," he yelled to the students who were standing, trying to see what was happening. "Nothing to see, so I want you to sit down, now!" his voice elevated.

Mumbling, they returned to their seats.

Stony Creek's volunteer fire department/ rescue team was on the scene within a half-hour. Most of the men and women in the team had other jobs but were on-call for an emergency.

Ernie Loomis was one of the volunteers. He knew it was Taylor when they got the call on the radio, but he was hoping that his friend wasn't dead.

He gathered his gear and ran over to Taylor, disentangling him from the tree and gently laid him out on the ground. "Hey pal," he said softly as he kneeled beside his friend, brushing tree bark from Taylor's face. "Why'd you have to go do something stupid like this, huh?" Tears flowed freely down his face.

Jigger Johnson, another volunteer, attempted to take Taylor's vitals, but Ernie pushed him aside. "I've got this," he told Jigger. He checked his friend's carotid artery for a pulse, put his head on his chest to see if he could hear his heart beating and when he didn't he started CPR.

Ernie was willing Taylor to live, one, two, three, four, five, breathe, but in his heart he knew that Taylor's injuries were too grave to sustain life.

Jigger stood next to Ernie, his hand on his shoulder, waiting for him to gain control of his emotions. After fifteen minutes of vigorous CPR, Ernie stopped and sat down next to his friend to wait for the sheriff.

CHAPTER TWENTY-SIX

TRIPP'S SHRILL BARK WOKE Meredith from her unplanned afternoon nap. She was just going to close her eyes for a few minutes to ward off the headache that had been plaguing her for most of the day. "Who's out there, boy?" she asked, dragging herself off the couch.

Tripp ran to the front door, wagging his tail excitedly. He let out another loud bark just before Meredith heard a knock.

"Be right there," she said. "Tripp, sit!"

She could see through the window that her visitor was Dakota. "Oh God, I look a fright." She ran a hand through her hair and straightened her rumpled clothes. "Hi, come on in. I didn't expect you," she said opening the door.

"I've got some news, bad news, and wanted to let you know before you heard it from anyone else."

"Is it Gramps?" she asked, turning pale and clutching her chest. She always knew this day would come, but she wasn't ready for it yet.

"Oh no, honey," he answered, taking her hands in his. "I'm so sorry I frightened you. It's Taylor. He was killed on his motorcycle a couple of hours ago."

Did he just call me honey? "Thank God! I didn't mean thank God Taylor is dead," she said, shaking her head. "I'm just so glad it's not Gramps. I can't say I'm surprised though."

"He'd been drinking and was on his way to see Carrie. She was scared and called the sheriff. Fortunately for her, he never made it there."

Meredith sat down on the couch, brought her knees up and slid her arms around them. "Does Carrie know?"

"Yes. Linda and Larry were at the scene. They went home with the Reverend and told her and the boys."

"How did she take it?"

"She's full of guilt. Says if she hadn't called the sheriff, he'd still be alive, although that's not true. Taylor would have gone there regardless. "

"He had a death wish, I think. He was trouble with a big T. He couldn't stand knowing that Carrie was done with him. She was the best thing he'd ever had in his life and he abused it."

Dakota sat down next to her. Tripp bumped his head on Dakota's arm, wanting a pat. Dakota obliged. "Want to go outside and play with Jake?" he asked Tripp.

Tripp was on his feet running to the door, barking and turning in circles before Dakota had the words out of his mouth. Opening the door for him, Jake stood on the other side waiting to play. "There you go." The two dogs ran down the porch steps and raced across the lawn. Tripp picked up a yellow Frisbee that was in the grass and Jake grabbed the other side. They were in the midst of a tug of war before Dakota closed the door.

"Can I get you something to drink?" Meredith asked.

"Nothing for me, thanks. I have to get back to work."

"I suppose we'll be hearing soon about funeral arrangements and all."

"I'll let you know if I hear anything." He moved to the couch and stood before her. "Meredith, stand up," he told her, holding out his hand. "Come on, stand up," he said, when she hesitated, a wicked little grin starting at the corners of his mouth.

Her breathing was a little unsteady when she took his hand and let him bring her to her feet.

He used a finger to raise her chin, his touch soft and gentle. He tucked a loose strand of hair behind her ear and then leaned forward, kissing her on the forehead. He released her and turned away.

Frustrated, Meredith grabbed him by the arm. "Hey, wait a damn minute. You're not going to just walk out of here after a measly little kiss on the forehead, are you?"

He turned around, his eyes full of desire. He put his hand on the back of her neck and pulled her face toward his. The tension between them was electric. He leaned forward and covered her mouth in a powerful kiss, leaving them both with a longing yet unfulfilled.

"Do you want to take this further?" he asked teasingly, running his hand down her back and brushing it along her backside. "It's your call."

Meredith hesitated. Before she could answer, he kissed her again, more passionately. He covered her lips with his, his tongue finding hers. When they broke apart, they were both panting like two dogs in heat. Without saying a word, Meredith took his hand and led him upstairs to her bedroom.

Standing in front of her, Dakota undid the buttons on her blouse. He unhooked her bra and looked at her with admiration. She followed his lead and unfastened his shirt. She ran her hands over his chest and hard belly, feeling his erection straining at the fabric as she unbuttoned his jeans. In one swift motion, her jeans were off and they were on the bed, making out like teenagers.

Eagerly they caressed, kissed and pleasured each other until they collapsed, panting heavily. They lay in each other's arms, cuddling until Dakota began exploring Meredith's body again. "Let's take it slow this time," he murmured in her ear. "I want to feel all of you and taste every inch of you." Meredith moaned softly, the only response she could force out at the time. She loved the feel of his hands on her. Their mouths and bodies felt as natural to each other as if they'd been together for years. He slid his hand down her back, pressing her against him.

"Relax, sweetheart. Let me do all the work." *Relax? If I were any more relaxed, I'd be a big puddle on the floor. Do whatever you want, Babe. Take me to places I've never been.* Her hand closed over his penis and she heard him take in a sharp breath.

A FEW HOURS LATER, THEY EMERGED from upstairs, spent, and satisfied. "Can I get you a cup of coffee or something?" Meredith asked, a little shaky, embarrassed and unsure of herself.

"I don't need a thing," he answered huskily. "I have everything I've ever wanted." He slipped his arms around her and rested his chin on her head. She could feel him getting aroused again so she gently pulled away from him.

"So, does this make us a couple?"

He reached for her again and tightened his arms around her waist. "I hope it does. I want it to."

"Me, too," she said, purring like a kitten, hugging him back.

"I really have to get back to work," he said, grinning like a Cheshire cat. He had never been so happy. "Can I see you tonight?"

"I'd like that. Dakota?"

"Yeah?"

"I love you." *There, I've said it.*

Dakota's heart kicked like a bucking bronco. He hugged her tightly before untangling her arms from his waist. Holding her away from him, he studied her intently before speaking. "Meredith, I've loved you all my life. To hear you say you love

144

me, too, has made me the happiest man in Montana, probably even the whole world." He kissed her gently. "I have to go now or I'll never leave."

"See you tonight," she called as he jumped off her front steps.

CHAPTER TWENTY-SEVEN

THE DAY OF TAYLOR'S FUNERAL WAS GLOOMY.
Carrie sat at her mother's kitchen table more confused than she
had ever been. Despite what people thought about Taylor and
the problems they had, she had loved him, in her own way.
Regardless of his faults, he loved her, too.

Taylor had an ego, but his biggest problem was the bottle.
When he drank, he became an ugly person, someone she didn't
recognize. Ever since the night the bull gored him in the leg, he
had become a different man. He had demons she would never
know about.

Over the years, she tried talking to him, but he would
never open up to her. Her mother told her to quit making
excuses for him. No one could help him but himself and he was
too much of a man to seek help.

Carrie couldn't stop feeling responsible for his death. She
kept telling herself that if she hadn't called the sheriff after she
talked to her mother, if she'd handled things differently… if, if,
if. She had to stop blaming herself. The what ifs were not going
to bring Taylor back.

With her finding a job, her decision to leave her husband,
and his son standing up to him, Taylor was drinking more and
lashing out to anyone in his way. Carrie and her parents' biggest
fear had been that sooner or later one of them would end up

dead. No matter what, she was now a widow and their sons were without a father.

She fixed a cup of coffee, but didn't have an appetite. From the bowls left on the table, she noticed the boys had eaten cereal for breakfast. Her parents would be back soon to take them to the church.

She rinsed out her cup and stared out the window over the sink. *I'm so fortunate to have my family, church, and friends,* she thought. They had taken up a collection to help defray the costs of the funeral and to help her get back on her feet. Until then she had no idea how she was going to cover the expenses.

In addition, Ernie and Jackson told her about Taylor's wishes. It made things easy because the money given to her was enough to pay for his cremation. Ernie and Jackson would take care of his ashes. She was happy to oblige them, although she had no idea what they were going to do with them.

Carrie heard a car pull into the driveway. "Boys, it's time to go."

At the church, it seemed like everyone in town had shown up. Carrie knew some came to pay their respects and others were probably there to make sure Taylor really *was* dead. He had been difficult to many people over the years and had burned a lot of bridges. There were also those that were there for the refreshments and later would meet at the local bar to party, telling tales about Taylor, his antics, and his drinking.

Taylor's funeral, officiated by Reverend Anderson, was short and sweet. No one made Taylor out to be more than he was, yet people were respectful. During the service, Carrie did not shed a single tear. She had cried enough over the years and now this chapter of her life was over. She had no regrets, but hoped in the future, *if* she ever fell in love again, she would not only listen to her heart, but her head as well.

After the funeral, as promised, Carrie gave Ernie and Jackson Taylor's ashes. She still had no idea what they were going to do with them. She knew that whatever their plan was, it was something that Taylor demanded they do.

Later that day, Ernie, Jackson, and Carrie's eldest son, Gage, drove to the Buffalo Jump over in Three Forks. The three men made their way up the path to the jump, Gage holding his father's urn. "Should we say something?" Ernie asked.

Jackson and Gage shook their heads. "Let's get it over with," Gage said, passing the cremains to Ernie.

Ernie opened the urn and began scattering the ashes over the jump. "Best to you, old Buddy. Rest peacefully."

SEVERAL DAYS LATER, Meredith called Carrie. "Hi, how are you doing?"

"I'm doing okay, thanks."

"I'm sorry about Taylor," she said. "I know he and I had our differences, but he was the father of your children and I respect that."

"Thanks, Meredith."

"I'm not going to keep you, but I wanted you to know you still have a job at the diner." Meredith wasn't sure, but she thought she heard Carrie crying. She added, "Oh, and take all the time you need before coming back to work."

Carrie's voice was barely audible, but Meredith heard her say, "Thanks for everything. You're a true friend."

Meredith hung up the phone. "It's time I got the diner open for business."

CHAPTER TWENTY-EIGHT

GRAND OPENING – 5:30AM

MEREDITH AND ANNA ARRIVED at the diner at 4AM.
They fired up the grills, brewed the coffee, and prepared for
opening day. Meredith was excited and pacing the kitchen while
Anna, in her usual calm manner, cooked up oatmeal and cut up
fresh fruit.

"Will you please calm down?" Anna scolded.
"Everything is going to be fine, just you wait and see."

Hearing a truck pull into the parking lot, Meredith looked
out the window. It was Dakota. The diner was still dark except
for the kitchen. She ran to the back door and opened it for him
throwing her arms around his neck. "I'm so happy to see you,"
she murmured, squeezing him tightly.

He pushed her back slightly, peering into her eyes. "You
nervous?" he asked with a grin.

"As a wet hen," she replied.

Dakota leaned forward and gave her a loving kiss.

Anna stirred the oatmeal, a knowing smile on her face.
*I'm so glad these kids are finally together. I knew one day
Meredith would realize how much she loves my son.*

"Hey, Ma," he said to Anna, putting his hands on her

shoulders and giving her a squeeze.

She didn't turn around but patted his hand. "Good morning, son. You're up early."

Dakota wasn't about to tell his mother he had spent the night at Meredith's. "Well, I thought maybe you ladies could use some help getting things ready."

"Oh, I see," Anna smiled, turned her head and lifted an eyebrow at her son.

Dakota felt a flush creep over his face. It reminded him of the time when he was a kid and was caught licking the icing off a cake. His mother always knew when he was lying.

Meredith stood watching the interaction between mother and son.

Anna was having a good time watching Dakota squirm and look at Meredith, why she was absolutely pale. No longer able to contain herself, Anna let out a loud laugh. "Do you two think you can put anything over on me? If you do, you'd better think again. Now let's get busy and get this diner open."

Before any of them could move, there was a loud knock on the back door. "I'll get it," Meredith said hurrying to unlock it, glad to be out from under Anna's knowing eye.

"Gramps, Sadie, come on in," she said enthusiastically.

"Thought you might need a little help this morning," Charlie said, ushering Sadie in before him.

"I'm pretty good in the kitchen, so if you need another cook, I'm willing," Sadie exclaimed.

"We can use all the help we can get," Meredith said, passing Sadie an apron.

At 4:45AM the waitresses arrived, Carrie Boone, Julia Loomis, and Sandra Weaver.

"Carrie, I hadn't expected you today," Meredith said. "How are you doing? It's good to see you."

"I couldn't let you down on opening day when you've

been so good to me," Carrie said, tears welling up in her eyes.

Meredith gave her a quick hug and then put the girls to work. "The creamers need to be filled, make sure the salt and pepper shakers are full, and the sugar bowls." She paused, glancing around. "And please, give the diner a quick once over to make sure everything looks perfect."

At precisely 5:30AM, Meredith turned the diner lights on. Unlocking the door, her eyes widened with amazement. A lively crowd was waiting outside in the chilly morning air. With a warm smile, she announced, "Welcome to Stony Creek Diner." They cheered, clapped their hands, and made their way inside.

Some settled into the booths while others sat at the counter. They plunked quarters into the little jukeboxes and within minutes, Stony Creek Diner was alive with music and hungry people.

The three waitresses worked fast and efficiently taking orders, pouring coffee, and serving the piping hot food to their customers.

Meredith, Anna, and Sadie worked steadily to keep up with the orders. *I'm going to have to hire a full-time cook to help keep up the pace,* she thought. Anna was only part-time.

Jigger Johnson and Willa Mae, closed the Powder Horn Café that morning. They respected Charlie and Meredith and wanted opening day to be successful for her. They also wanted to see their competition up close and personal.
"This is such a unique place," Willa said to Jigger. "It's so different than our café I doubt we'll have to worry about Meredith taking our customers."

After the first rush, the diner quieted down. Business remained steady but not crazy as it had been in the early morning hours.

An 18-wheeler pulled into the parking lot. The driver got

out and stood looking at the diner, trying to decide what to do. He knew what he wanted to do, but he wondered if he could he pull it off? No matter, he had to try.

Lowering the visor on his baseball cap, he walked up the parking lot driveway, head low, hands in his jacket pockets. He'd let his facial hair grow into a full beard to avoid being recognized. Walking into the welcoming warmth of the diner, he took a seat at the farthest end of the counter.

Julia hurried over to him and smiled. "Howdy. Coffee?" she asked, holding up the pot to him.

"Yes, please." He picked up a menu that was standing between the salt and pepper shakers.

"Take a few minutes and I'll be back for your order."

The man nodded. *What the hell am I doing here? Am I crazy or what? But I have to see...*

Charlie got up from the back booth and sauntered over to the counter when he saw the man come in. He'd seen this guy a few times in town, but no one seemed to know who he was. He took a seat next to him.

"Mornin'," he said.

"Hey," the man grunted, head low over his coffee as he took a sip. He didn't look in Charlie's direction. His heart was pounding so hard in his chest that he felt sure the older man sitting next to him could hear it.

"New around these parts?" Charlie asked.

"Just passing through. I'm a trucker."

"Ah," Charlie said. "I thought I saw you in town a few times." He stared at the man. There was something about him, but Charlie couldn't put his finger on it. His profile and voice were vaguely familiar. A flicker of recognition went through him. Could it be?

He was about to question the man further when Meredith

came out of the kitchen.

God, she looked beautiful, the man thought. *His heart ached to reach out and touch her, but he couldn't. It had been way too long. She'd never forgive him.*

"Hey, Gramps. Can you believe how many people showed up for the opening? I was overwhelmed," she grinned.

"I know, honey. It was a wonderful turnout. You should be proud."

"I don't know why I ever thought this diner was a crazy idea. I guess Velvet knew what she was doing all along."

The man felt a twinge of sadness at the mention of Velvet's name. He inhaled deeply and let it out slowly.

Charlie glanced in his direction. Who was this guy and what was it about him that was gnawing at him so?

Julia returned. "Can I take your order now?" She glanced over at Charlie. "You want a little more coffee?"

"No thanks."

"I'll have another coffee to go," the stranger said. "I need to get back on the road."

"You sure you don't want a muffin or anything?"

"Just the check if you don't mind."

"Sure thing." She wrote up his check, ripped it off the pad and laid it on the counter. She filled a Styrofoam container with coffee and put a lid on it. She passed it to the man. "Make sure you come back again," she added with a smile, walking over to another customer.

"I'll do that." He glanced at the check, put his money on the counter and slid off the stool.

"Mister!" Charlie said.

The trucker turned and looked at Charlie. Their eyes held for a moment before the man turned away. As quick as he could, he strode to the diner's front door and made his exit.

By God, it is him! Charlie felt like he'd been punched in the gut. After the shock of recognizing the man, Charlie jumped off his stool and followed the tall, broad shouldered male figure out the door. "Dallas!"

The man stopped for a brief moment before hurrying on.

From the diner's door, Meredith stood watching the scenario unfold. Hand to her chest she screamed, "Oh my God."

The customers sat in silence watching Meredith as she ran out the door. She ran down the steps and stood next to her grandfather.

"DADDY?"

CHAPTER TWENTY-NINE

"DADDY? IS IT REALLY YOU?" Meredith called to the man again. Crying and shaking uncontrollably, she felt her grandfather gather her into a bear hug, preventing her from running down the driveway.

Charlie knew in his heart the stranger was his long-lost son-in-law, Dallas Banning, but he wasn't about to let his granddaughter run after him. Dallas was the one who deserted Meredith so many years ago, and Charlie, fiercely protective, was going to make sure she didn't get hurt again. If Dallas wanted a reunion with his daughter, then he would have to make the first move or the reunion would never work.

The man stopped at the bottom of the driveway and hesitated before taking off his baseball cap. Slowly he turned around and started walking toward his father-in-law and daughter. His heart was pounding and his breathing was uneven. His eyes flooded with tears and threatened to overflow. *How could he defend his reasons for leaving Stony Creek? When he explained would it be enough for her to forgive him?* He wondered.

Meredith broke loose from her grandfather's grip and ran toward the man, arms outstretched. Dallas picked up his pace

155

and met his daughter mid-way, embracing her with a powerful hug.

"Little girl, I've missed you so much," he whispered into her ear.

Pulling away, Meredith stared at him. "I can't believe it's you, Daddy." She blasted him with several quick questions. "Where did you go? Why didn't you stay in touch with me? How did you know I was back in Stony Creek?"

His eyes were pleading with her to understand, those wonderful kind, brown eyes that she would have known anywhere. He had protected her from Velvet's cruelty all the years she was growing up, but a year after Meredith left home he had mysteriously dropped off the face of the earth.

Now that he was here, she needed to touch him, to smell his scent, to make sure he was real and not some figment of her imagination. She ran her hands over his face, through his hair, up and down his arms, and suddenly, from the deep recesses of her being, anger rose up inside her and boiled over. Without warning, she drew her hand back and slapped him as hard as she could across his face. Howling like a wounded animal, she began to beat on his chest.

Dallas did nothing to restrain her. He deserved everything she was dishing out and if it would make her feel better, then he would let her rail on him.

Charlie ran down the driveway and grabbed Meredith around the waist, pulling her off Dallas. "That's enough!" he ordered.

Feet dangling off the ground, she continued flailing around and Charlie tightened his grip. "Meredith! Stop it right now!"

Her grandfather's words finally got through to her and she stopped struggling. Charlie carefully let loose of her.

Slowly, Meredith sank to the ground, sobs catching in her throat.

Dallas remained where he was. Seeing his daughter's devastation, he felt incredibly guilty, as if he had just kicked a small puppy.

Peering over the top of his glasses at his son-in-law, Charlie's bushy white brows drew together in a scowl. "So it *is* you!" he barked. "I can't believe you've been skulking around town all these months instead of being a man and facing up to your daughter. What the hell you gonna' do now? Leave again? 'Cause if that's what you're planning, leave now," he demanded, leaning down to stroke Meredith's hair. She was hanging onto her grandfather's legs, much like a baby wanting protection.

Before Dallas could respond, a blur of denim flew past Charlie and Meredith. A fist connected with Dallas's mid-section causing him to keel over backward, rolling a few feet before coming to a stop.

"You stay right there," Dakota yelled, standing over the man and pointing his finger at him. All he knew was his girl was on the ground and this man had something to do with it.

Wide-eyed, Meredith unwrapped herself from her grandfather's legs and scrambled to her feet. "Dakota stop!" she cried, grabbing him by the arm. "Don't hurt him. He's my father."

"Oh shit." Confused, he glanced over at her. "Are you sure?"

She nodded.

He leaned over the man lying on the ground and offered him a hand up. "Sorry about that," he said, pulling Dallas to his feet.

"It's been a long time, Dakota," Dallas groaned, hanging onto his stomach.

Meredith ran over to her father. "Are you okay, Daddy?"

"I'm fine," he told her. "He didn't pack nearly the wallop you did, little girl," Dallas chuckled, rubbing the side of his face where his daughter had slapped him.

"I don't know what came over me. I'm so sorry."

"Don't apologize for anything, little girl. I had it coming."

"You didn't answer Gramps. What are you going to do now? Are you going to stay?"

"How do you feel about it?"

"Nothing would make me happier." She turned to her grandfather. "What do you say, Gramps?"

Charlie blew his nose with a loud honking sound. He was a sentimental old fool and on the brink of tears seeing how happy his granddaughter was. He gave Meredith the answer he knew she wanted.

"It's okay with me. I've always had a soft spot for your dad. He's a good guy and it will be great to have him home."

CHAPTER THIRTY

"LET'S GO GET SOME BREAKFAST," Charlie said, giving Dallas a friendly slap on the back. "I've worked up another appetite after all this."

"Great idea, Gramps," Meredith said. "I'm famished. You hungry, Dad?"

"I think I could eat now," he responded, placing his arm around his daughter and hugging her close. "I nearly strangled to death earlier on my coffee when your granddad sat down next to me."

Meredith flashed him a grin and put her arm around his waist. How good it felt to have him near her. She remembered the times they had walked like this when she was a little girl.

When Velvet would go on her rants, accusing Meredith of never doing anything right, Meredith would cry and run outside, hands over her ears to shut out her mother's voice. Dallas would come to her rescue, hug her tightly and make her feel like she was the most special person in the world, just like he made her feel today.

When they reached the top of the driveway, to their surprise, most of the customers were standing outside. They'd been watching the scene unfold. Loud cheers rang out when they stepped aside to let the four enter the diner.

Anna ran up to Dallas and gave him a hearty hug. Her face broke into a welcoming smile. "Welcome home, Dallas. It's been too long. Yuma is going to be so happy to see you."

Dallas, overcome with emotion, hugged her back. He couldn't utter a word or he'd be bawling like a baby in front of all these folks. The people that meant the most were welcoming him home with open arms, non-judging, just happy to have him back, especially his daughter.

After they entered the diner, they seated themselves in a booth. Julia hurried over to them, four mugs in one hand and the coffee pot in the other. "Coffee everyone?" she said brightly.

"All the way around," Charlie gestured his finger in a circle. "This has certainly been an exciting morning."

Julia filled their coffee mugs and passed each one of them a menu. "I'll give you all a chance to look the menu over and I'll be back in a few minutes."

"You can stay with me, Dad, if you want. I'm living at our old house. There's plenty of room."

Dakota glanced at her, eyes questioning, after he heard her invite Dallas to stay at the house. Meredith understood what he was asking. He needed confirmation that nothing was going to change between them now that her father was back. She reached over and put her hand on top of his, assuring him that everything was going to be okay.

"Dad, just thought you should know Dakota and I are more than friends," she said, grinning at Dakota. "He's around a lot when he's not working."

"That doesn't surprise me. He's been in love with you since he was a teenager," Dallas said, remembering how Dakota used to defend his daughter.

Julia returned to the table for their orders. "Have you decided yet?"

"I'll start with a bowl of oatmeal," Charlie said. "I also want three eggs, over easy, five strips of bacon, and home fries with onions, wheat toast, and orange juice."

"I'd like a stack of flapjacks with maple syrup and bacon," Dallas told her. "And more coffee, please."

"I'll just have an order of English muffins," Meredith said.

"We have some fresh blueberry muffins today that Anna just took out of the oven. Interested?" she asked her boss.

"That does sound good. I'll have the muffin instead. Will you have her grill mine?" Meredith was pleased that Julia was trying to promote different items on the menu. She'd have to commend her for that.

"Dakota? You ready to order?" Julia asked.

"I've already eaten and I have to get to work," he said, squeezing his way out of the booth. He leaned over and gave Meredith a light kiss on her cheek. "I'll catch you all later."

"Charlie Parker, are you trying to kill yourself?" Sadie shouted as she flew out of the kitchen, shaking his order slip at him. "Eggs, bacon, home fries? Humph! That's a heart attack waiting to happen, but it won't be happening this morning if I have anything to say about it. You'll have oatmeal and orange juice and that will be it!"

"Now Sadie," Charlie said. "We're having a celebration here. Don't go spoiling it trying to keep me alive. If I die today, I'll die a happy man."

"Well, you're not going to die today so oatmeal it will be." Sadie turned on her heel and stomped back to the kitchen.

Arguing with Sadie was impossible. He looked at his granddaughter and Dallas and shook his head. "Ever since I told that woman I'm in love with her, she's become an old bossy-boots, watching everything I eat, drink, or do. If I didn't love her so much I'd tell her to go shit in her hat!"

Meredith and Dallas burst out laughing. "That's quite a visual, Gramps," she said and laughed again.

"I haven't heard that expression in years," Dallas chuckled.

"Well, it's true. Where the hell *is* my oatmeal anyway?" he demanded, slapping the table with the palm of his hand, a half-smirk on his face. As much as he disliked Sadie bossing him around, Charlie adored her and loved it when she made a fuss over him. *I'm going to have to marry that girl one of these days.*

Julia hurried over to Charlie with his bowl of oatmeal. "Here you go, Charlie," she said.

"Thanks for ratting me out," he sputtered.

"I did no such thing, Charlie Parker. I placed my orders and it didn't take Sadie long to figure out who was eating what."

"That's what you say," he muttered, pretending not to believe a word she was saying. Pouring a little cream on his oatmeal, he glanced over his shoulder at the small diamond-shaped window in the kitchen door. Not seeing Sadie, he sprinkled four packets of brown sugar on his cereal.

"I saw that Charlie Parker," she yelled from the kitchen.

"Damn," he said. He drove his spoon into the oatmeal much as a farmer drives a shovel into a pile of manure and with just as little pleasure. Charlie wanted bacon and eggs. Oatmeal wasn't cutting it.

"I won't be coming back here to eat breakfast," he yelled back. "Not as long as you're in the kitchen anyway."

"Oh Gramps, relax," Meredith said, patting him on the hand. "She's just looking out for you and wants to keep you around a long time."

Julia came back to the table with the rest of the orders and set them in front of Dallas and Meredith. Dallas lathered his flapjacks with butter and poured a hearty amount of maple syrup over them. He was about to take the first bite when….."

"You sure *that* isn't a heart attack waiting to happen?" Charlie asked sarcastically, pointing at the stack of pancakes.

Dallas eyed his father-in-law closely. "Charlie. Is that a bit of drool I see in the corner of your mouth?" he chuckled, passing him a napkin.

"Oh hell," Charlie said, slapping the napkin aside. He slammed his spoon down and stood up. "I'm leaving. I'm going to the Powder Horn where a person can get a decent breakfast around here," he said loud enough so *someone* in the kitchen could hear him.

"Gramps, don't go. Dad's only having a little fun with you, and besides, the Powder Horn isn't open this morning."

"Too many people have been having fun with me today and I'm starving. Guess I'll go home and make my own eggs." He slammed his Stetson down onto his head so hard it hit his eyebrows and his ears popped out on both sides. Just before leaving, he turned to Dallas who had a huge grin on his face. "By the way pancake boy, make sure you leave Julia a big fat tip from me."

CHAPTER THIRTY-ONE

MEREDITH SIPPED HER COFFEE while watching her father eat his breakfast. It had been twenty years since she'd shared a meal with him. It all seemed unreal to her. She took a bite of her grilled muffin. "Yum," she said, licking her lips and savoring the taste. "Anna makes the best blueberry muffins of anyone I know."

Dallas looked up from his flapjacks. He knew his daughter had been watching him. *I have to tell her I won't be staying. Will she think I'm going to bail on her again, or will she believe me when I tell her I'll be back?*

How long have you known I was in Stony Creek?" she asked.

"Ever since you got here," he admitted. "I've kind of kept track of you over the years, which is why I started long-distance trucking."

"You've been here ever since I've been here?" she asked, incredulously.

"Not all the time," he answered. "Only when I had a job that brought me to this part of Montana. Several nights I camped out in the diner because it made me feel close to you."

"How did you get in?"

164

"The latch on the back door was broken. Someone else had been squatting here before me. I changed the lock so no one else could break in."

"So it was you?" she asked, remembering the day she found the wrinkled piece of paper on the floor of the diner. When she picked it up, the paper turned out to be an old, worn photograph of Meredith and Velvet. "That photo freaked me out when I found it. I thought someone was stalking me."

"I carried that picture in my jacket pocket for years. I'd lie in my bunk at night looking at my pretty, teenage daughter remembering how much I love you. Then I'd look at your mother. She was always beautiful in my eyes and I adored her, but she was a difficult woman to love. When you left home, there was no reason for me to stay. She drove us both away from her."

Meredith sat quietly listening to her father, thinking what a sorry mess his marriage must have been. Velvet didn't miss a chance to show how much she hated being a mother, so Meredith could only imagine how she was as a wife.

"Honey, you asked me a while ago if I'd come and stay with you at the house," he said, wiping his mouth on his napkin.

"Well, what do you think?" Meredith asked. "We have so much to catch up on. It'll be wonderful to have coffee with you in the mornings and dinner together every evening."

"The fact is, Meredith, it's not that simple." He frowned into his coffee and took a sip. "I have commitments I need to take care of first. I have a few more jobs to finish up before I can stop trucking. People are depending on me. I hope you'll understand."

Meredith's face turned ashen. The happiness in her eyes dimmed. He was telling her he was going to leave again. His obligations to others meant more to him than his allegiance to her. She couldn't bear rejection again, at least not by the only parent she had. She scrambled up from the table, knocking over her coffee cup and ran toward the kitchen, flashing him an accusing look over her shoulder.

Dallas stood up. "Meredith, wait," he called after her.

"What's wrong?" Sadie and Anna asked when Meredith kicked the kitchen door open and marched in

"He's leaving!" she spat, stamping her feet on the floor, like a child throwing a tantrum.

The door swung open and Dallas hurried into the room to face his daughter. Sadie and Anna hovered closer to Meredith, circling her like a wagon train, protecting her from what Dallas was about to say.

"I *will* be back," he said soothingly, imploring her to trust him. "I don't know what else to say to make you believe me. I guess you'll just have to have faith in me, only I can understand why that might be difficult." He moved close to Meredith, gave her a hug, and placed a quick kiss on her cheek.

She stood her ground, stubborn, not giving in, even though she felt like she was dying inside. She wanted to believe him, knew he deserved a second chance, but she was afraid he'd leave and not come back.

"I'll be going now." He looked at Sadie and Anna. "Please take care of my little girl until I get back."

Anna whispered into Meredith's ear. "Don't bite off your nose to spite your face. You might regret it."

She took Anna's words to heart, giving it merit before she spoke. "Dad?"

Dallas stopped and turned to look at his daughter. "Will you really come back?"

"I promise, and until I do, I'll call you every day. Can I have a hug?"

166

Meredith nodded and walked into her father's open arms. "Hurry back," she cried, holding him tightly.

"I'll be back before you know it," he said. Tears of happiness filled his eyes as he left the diner.

"Well, this has been one heck of an opening day," Sadie commented.

"You'd better go freshen up," Anna said to Meredith. "Wipe your tears, wash your face, and comb your hair. Now get going."

"Yes, ma'am," Meredith said. She smiled walking toward the washroom. Anna had been more of a mother to her than Velvet ever had been, and when she spoke, Meredith paid attention. After pulling herself together, she went back to the kitchen. She put her arms around Anna embracing her lovingly. "Thanks, Anna. I needed that."

"Get on with you now," she said, shooing Meredith away.

MEREDITH WENT BACK OUT to the diner to check on the waitresses and her customers. It was quiet now except for a few locals drinking coffee and chatting with friends. She poured herself a glass of milk, picked up the Stony Creek Daily, and hunkered down in one of the back booths. She was exhausted after a busy and emotional morning.

She waved when she saw Reverend Anderson come in and take a seat at the end of the counter. "Hey, Meredith," he called to her. "I heard you had a great opening this morning.

"We sure did. Good to see you."

Carrie Boone took a menu over to him. "Morning, Reverend. Care for some coffee?

"I'd love some, Carrie. How are you doing?"

Carrie set a mug of steaming coffee in front of him. "Cream?"

"Just black for me. So how *are* you doing?"

"I'm doing okay," she said softly. "It's been hard on the boys, especially Danny. He loved his father so much."

"I'd be happy to talk to him if you think it would help," he offered.

"Well, I'll see how it goes. If he doesn't perk up in a bit, I'll let you know."

"You make sure you do. I'm available whenever you need me."

Gosh he's good looking. What am I thinking? My husband's been dead only a month and I'm ogling the reverend. "Are you ready to order?" she asked, hoping he wouldn't notice her shaking hands.

She's cuter than a bug's ear, he thought, *and she's changed so much since Taylor died. Slimmer, more confident, and what a beautiful smile she has. Why didn't I notice it before now? Maybe it was because she never smiled.* Storm had dated a few women over the years, but never found the right girl to marry. He was still Stony Creek's most eligible bachelor.

Grinning like a schoolboy he said, "I guess I'll have scrambled eggs, bacon, wheat toast, and tomato juice."

She blushed as he studied her while she wrote his order. "I'll get this right away," she said, hurrying to the kitchen.

Meredith watched the interaction between the reverend and Carrie, sensing a possible connection brewing between the two of them. As she'd gotten to know Carrie better, she discovered what a sweet person she was. Carrie needed a strong, dependable man in her life, and the reverend needed a warm, caring woman in his.

THE BIG, GREEN SEMI BARRELED down the road past the diner. Dallas pulled on the air horn and waved to his daughter.

Meredith ran outside waving good-bye. She smiled,

Stony Creek Diner

knowing in her heart that he would be back this time.

CHAPTER THIRTY-TWO

A STRANGE SOUND ROUSED MEREDITH. Half-awake, she puzzled for a moment, then feeling chilly, snuggled closer to a softly snoring Dakota. There was that sound again. She rolled over and checked to see Tripp lying on the floor sound asleep.

Jake, the sly rascal, had crawled up onto the bed during the night. He lay there sprawled across the bottom with his feet splayed out behind him, not a care in the world. Apparently, nothing had bothered either dog.

Confused by the continuous sound, Meredith pushed back the covers and padded across the room. Snow was tapping gently on the window. When she looked closer, she noticed the ground was covered, sparkling like tiny diamonds.

Excited, she ran back to the bed and jostled Dakota. He mumbled something unintelligible and burrowed deeper into the comfort of the bed. "Come look," she said, shaking him. "It's snowing. I haven't seen snow in years. Let's go outside."

Dakota sat up, sleepy-eyed. He looked at her as if she had three heads, groaned and threw himself back on his pillow.

She pulled the covers off him, playfully slapping his naked backside. "Come on, Dakota. Get up and come outside with me," she whined, putting one leg into her jeans and then the other. She grabbed a sweatshirt off the chair and pulled it on over her head. She gave Jake a playful pat on the butt. "Get up you lazy old dog. We're going out to play." Barefoot she hurried to the stairs, Tripp at her heels.

Jake slowly slithered off the edge of the bed. On his feet, he shook himself, stretched and let out a big yawn.

"Oh for goodness sake," she admonished the large dog. "You and your master are no fun at all."

She walked back to the bed. "Are you coming?" she asked the naked body that was still lying prone on her bed.

"I'd much prefer it if you would crawl back in next to me," he grumbled, reaching for her.

"Later," she said, pushing his hand away. "Right now I'm going to go see the snow."

She ran down the stairs, grabbed her coat off the hook, and slid her sockless feet into her boots. She threw on her Stetson and shoved her fingers into her gloves.

Opening the door, she stepped outside onto the porch. Meredith drew in a breath at the scene before her. The sky was gray as gunmetal and the snowflakes were coming down harder. She ran down the steps feeling the snow landing softly on her face, tickling her nose. She laid her head back and stuck out her tongue so a few flakes could land on it. When they did, she giggled like a child.

The trees were blowing restlessly, trying to shake off the wet intrusion covering their branches. The mountains, obstructed by the weather, were invisible to her. Coming from Gramps' direction, the smell of wood smoke, so thick she could almost taste it, assailed her nostrils. *He must have stoked up the old wood stove.*

The two dogs hadn't ventured forth and were still standing on the porch. "Come on, Tripp, Jake," she said, slapping her legs to get their attention. "Let's go play in the snow."

Tripp had never seen snow before. He ran after Meredith stopping in his tracks when the white stuff covered his feet. Sniffing the ground, his nose filled with snow. He shook his head and let out a loud sneeze. Jake went bounding around Tripp, nose to the ground burrowing a trough as he went through the snow. Deciding that this cold stuff might be fun after all, Tripp went running after his old buddy.

Meredith ran all over the yard, kicking the snow into the air, making snowballs, and finally falling on her back. Childhood memories overwhelmed her while she swished her arms and legs back and forth making a snow angel.

At the first snow of the season, Meredith and her dad would walk into the silent woods, hearing only their boots crunching on the crisp new snow as they looked for animal tracks, leaving their own fresh prints behind them.

Back at the house, they'd lie down in the fresh snow, side by side, and make snow angels. Later they'd make a snowman and dress him up with a cowboy hat, a knitted scarf, and a carrot for his nose. Grandma, who'd been watching from the window, would come running out, her feet shoved into Gramps's boots and hair flying every which way. "Wait, he's not finished yet. He needs eyes," she hollered, thrusting two large buttons into Meredith's snow covered mittens.

When their fingers and toes were numb from the cold, they'd go back in the house and sit at the kitchen table. Meredith's favorite part of the day was sharing with her dad a large mug of hot chocolate with three fat marshmallows floating on the top. How she wished her father were here this morning.

The two dogs ran back to Meredith when she fell. They licked her face and grabbed at her gloves, trying to pull her up.

"I'm okay, I'm okay," she laughed and threw snow on them. They shook furiously and covered her with the same snow.

"Okay, boys, I give up. Let's go back inside. I think I need some hot chocolate." She stood up and brushed off the snow. Glancing at the house, she saw Dakota standing on the porch, leaning against the post, arms crossed over his bare chest.

"Are you all done playing?" he called out to her, shivering. He hadn't expected to be outside so long or he would have put on a jacket. She was having such a good time, maybe he should have taken her up on her offer.

"I'll be right in," she answered. She had a terrible urge to throw a snowball at him, but since he was half-naked, she thought better of it. Oh, what the heck. She decided to do it anyway. She reached down and grabbed a fistful of snow, rolled it into a tight little ball, squinted one eye and took aim at Dakota.

"You're going to be sorry if you do it," he warned, backing away. He pointed his finger at her. "Don't you do it, Meredith. I'm not kidding." Trying to be stern, he couldn't help smiling. She had a wicked gleam in her eye and was about to unload that ball of snow on him.

Grinning she ran forward and heaved the snowball, hitting him square on his bare chest.

Damn it was cold. Growling, he jumped down the steps. Meredith squealed loudly, turned and ran the other way. Before she got more than a few feet away, Dakota's muscled body tackled her from behind, hurling her to the ground. He grabbed a handful of snow and rubbed it all over her face. "Take that you wench," he said triumphantly.

"No fair," she cried out, grabbing some snow in her gloves and getting him right back.

Pinning her arms down Dakota bent over her, his body wet and glistening, drops of snow falling from his hair onto her face. His dark eyes sparkled as he kissed the tip of her nose and ran his cold hand under her shirt, making her nipples rise to the occasion. He wanted to take her, right here in the front yard, but

173

it was freezing and so was he. He dropped back on his knees and reached for her, pulling her to him. "I love you more than you'll ever know, Meredith," he said, hugging her to his chest.

She nuzzled his neck. "I love you, too, Dakota. I'm yours forever if you want me." She meant it, never dreaming that life would be so good for her.

"Let's get back inside," he said, pulling her to her feet. "I'm frozen and we both have to get to work."

They hurried up the steps and into the house, shaking off the snow sticking to their clothes and boots. "Coffee's made," he said, walking to the kitchen.

Meredith found a towel and wiped down the two wet dogs who were still bouncing around from the excitement. "Go lay down," she said, pointing to the kitchen.

"I got a call from Harry Goodfellow when you were outside," Dakota went on as he poured them each a cup of the steaming brew.

"Who's he?" Meredith asked, blowing into her coffee before tasting it. She still wanted hot chocolate, but she'd wait until she got to the diner.

"He's a good friend of mine and another warden. I'll be gone for a couple of days. A black bear near Gardiner has been breaking into unlocked vehicles the past couple of weeks. He's become a nuisance. Probably a yearling let loose by his mother. We need to find him, trap him, and relocate him before someone gets hurt. If people would just lock their vehicles like they're instructed to do this wouldn't be a problem."

"Jake can stay here with us while you're gone," she said.

"I'm taking him with me. It's easier to track a bear when you have a dog with you. They get on the scent and lead you right to them."

"Please be careful," she said, wrapping her arms around his waist and settling herself against his body so that her breasts caressed his chest.

She heard him suck in a breath and she smiled. What a heady feeling to make a big, strong man melt like a marshmallow.

"I will." He gave her a kiss on top of her head. "I need to get ready now." She felt his desire as he unwound himself from her embrace and went upstairs to get dressed.

Meredith called the diner to let the girls know she'd be a little late. She ran up to her bedroom after him with one thought in mind. She was going to make crazy love to Dakota before he left to fight off a bear.

CHAPTER THIRTY-THREE

MEREDITH AND DAKOTA LAY SPENT after a quick, but hot and heavy lovemaking session. "You've created a monster," she purred, nuzzling his neck, "but it's time to get up." On second thought, she kissed him, again, seeking his tongue with her own.

"Oh no you don't," he grinned, pushing her away. "You're trying to kill me and doing a good job of it, too." He leapt out of bed and she scooted after him to the bathroom.

Showering together and after another round of gymnastic sex, they dressed and went downstairs for one more cup of coffee before he had to leave. The snow continued to fall and the wind started picking up. Dakota began pacing and glanced out the window. "I'd better be heading out. I've got quite a drive ahead of me."

"Please be careful," she told him, standing up from the table to hug him. He took her by the shoulders and lowered his mouth to hers, kissing her deeply. His kiss left her breathless, wanting more and he knew it, but he gently moved her aside, ruffling her hair. "I'll be back, don't you worry. I have some unfinished business here." He slapped her playfully on the butt. "Come on, Jake. Let's go get us a bear."

Meredith watched as he pulled out of the driveway and headed down the road. It was time for her to go work. She felt a tad guilty leaving her staff to fend for themselves so she could have some hot sex with her boyfriend, but giggling, not that guilty. Pushing the thought aside, she shrugged into her L.L.Bean jacket, thrust her feet into her boots and pulled on her gloves. She added a wool scarf to her attire, wrapping it loosely around her neck.

Pussyfooting her way to the barn where she parked the truck, she covered her nose with the scarf to ward off the cold and the snow. Pulling the barn doors open was not an easy job with snow flying everywhere. She tugged at the double doors. They creaked in protest as the ice gave way from the hardware and eventually opened.

She hurried inside, away from the frigid air. She scrambled into her truck and turned the ignition. It turned right over. *I doubt Mercedes would have been this kind.* She put the truck in gear and slowly pulled out of the barn, stopping to jump out and close the barn doors.

She turned on the heater and defroster. *Why did I ever think moving back to Montana was such a good idea?* Unaccustomed to the slippery roads, she drove all the way to town at a snail's pace, fearful she would slide off into the ditch.

After what seemed like an eternity, she pulled into the diner's driveway. Stepping from her truck, her feet slipped out from under her and down she went. "Owwww," she yelped. Lying on her back, she cautiously moved her arms and legs, hoping that nothing was broken.

Reverend Anderson was heading up the driveway when he noticed Meredith lying on the ground. "Are you hurt?" he asked, reaching down to help her.

"Only my pride," she said, embarrassed, giving him her hand. "Thanks. I haven't driven in snow in a long time. Obviously I haven't walked in it either," she said dryly, brushing

177

the snow off her clothes. "It's only the middle of October. Isn't it early for this much snow, or any snow for that matter?"

"It is a bit early, but snow can occur anytime from early October on. I don't think this will last."

"I'm sure glad I got rid of Mercedes. She wouldn't have enjoyed the ride to town this morning. I think my truck could drive through an avalanche. It's great in the snow."

They walked into the diner together, stomping their snow-covered boots on the welcome mat. Meredith greeted the regulars and walked behind the counter to make a mug of hot chocolate. She'd been craving one all morning after her romp in the snow and in the hay.

Reverend Anderson walked to the counter where Carrie was serving. He slid onto the stool and waited.

She blushed slightly before she smiled at him. Her face felt hot and she hoped he wouldn't notice. "Morning Reverend. What can I do for you?"

"Morning, Carrie. The first thing you can do is stop calling me reverend. Call me Storm, please."

"Oh, I don't know if I could do that, Reverend." Flustered by his attention, she grabbed a cloth and starting wiping down the counter top, stopping to fill a mug with black coffee and placing it before him.

"So you remembered I like my coffee black." He smiled at her. "Now, back to whether or not you could call me by my first name, sure you could. We've been friends for years."

Ignoring him, she went on, "Do you want breakfast or lunch? The specials are elk stew or pan fried brown trout." Order pad and pencil ready, she stood facing him, tapping her foot nervously.

Storm inhaled deeply, afraid that what he was about to say would scare her away, but he had to take the chance. "Carrie?"

"You ready?" she smiled sweetly, pencil poised.

"Carrie, would you go to dinner with me some evening?"

Startled, she dropped the pad and pencil. Bending down to pick them up, she took a second to regain her composure. After years of living with Taylor, she had little self-esteem and here this handsome man was asking her on a date. She stood up, eyes widened with surprise as she faced him. "Are you serious?"

"Is it so difficult for you to believe a man would want to take you on a date? You're a beautiful woman, Carrie. It's just dinner. What do you say?"

"I'd say you better place your order before I get in trouble. About the other thing, I'll think about it," she said shyly.

Heart hammering in her chest, she couldn't believe Reverend Anderson had asked her out. Shocked wasn't the word for it. He could have knocked her over with a feather.

She took a minute to think about it. He had become a regular, making sure he sat where she was serving. Maybe he'd been flirting with her all along, although she couldn't say for sure. She hadn't been alone with another man since she was fifteen and wouldn't even know how to act. Maybe she could get some advice from Meredith. She wondered if she should tell her mother. Was it too soon after Taylor's death?

"Home fries, toast…ah, earth to Carrie," he said, bringing her back to reality.

"What? Oh, I'm sorry, Rev… er, Storm. My mind was somewhere else. Would you please give me your order again?"

With an easy grin on his face, Storm repeated his breakfast order, pleased that Carrie called him by his given name. He knew he had Carrie's attention and had given her something to think over. He'd admired her from afar for a long time, even when she was married to Taylor. Her life hadn't been an easy one, but if he had his way, he'd see to it that no one ever hurt her again.

SANDRA WEAVER LOVED TO COOK, not waitress. However, it was a job and she was grateful to be working. One particularly busy morning a few weeks earlier, Sandra noticed Meredith working feverishly trying to fill the breakfast orders in a timely fashion. Anna had the day off. Sandra stuck her head through the order window. "If you let me," she said, "I'm a good cook. I'd be happy to help you."

Desperate, Meredith agreed. "Come on in then, and we'll see what you can do." Within a few minutes, the women worked out a routine and orders started flying from the kitchen into the diner almost as quick as the waitresses placed them. Meredith offered her a job as a full-time cook the very same day with a nice raise in pay. Sandra was overjoyed with the opportunity to do what she liked to do best.

Business at the diner was doing great, better than Meredith would have imagined. They were in their second month and most days the diner was full for breakfast and lunch. In fairness to the Powder Horn Café, she closed the diner at 2pm every day. The Powder Horn's business hadn't suffered much, but this left them open for all the dinner folks. It also gave her staff a chance to get home early to be with their families.

ENTERING THE KITCHEN, Meredith greeted her newest cook. "Hey, Sandra, been busy this morning?"

"Steady, but nothing I couldn't handle. Anna was here for a couple of hours. She made some bread and cranberry walnut muffins and threw an elk stew together, which is simmering for the lunch crowd." Sandra noticed Meredith's afterglow and gave her the 'I know what you've been doing look'.

Meredith ignored her. "Mmmm, I can smell it," she said, inhaling the delicious aroma of the meat and vegetables.

"Anna left an hour ago saying she had to tend to Charlie and Yuma."

"She has the idea that those two men can't walk across a room without her directing them," Meredith laughed. "She takes good care of them and they enjoy it."

"I haven't seen Dakota around lately," Sandra said innocently, while the women sliced up veggies for salads and sandwiches. She looked over at her boss and watched Meredith's cheeks turn a lovely shade of pink. *Aha, I knew it!*

"He went up to Gardiner this morning, north of Yellowstone, to round up some rogue bear. I expect he'll back in a couple of days."

"The weatherman said Yellowstone got a lot of snow and it was still coming down."

"Well, it's still coming down here, too. I sure hope it lets up soon. I'm not used to this."

"Have you heard from Dallas?" Sandra asked making small talk. She wondered if she should be so nosy, but considered Meredith a friend now, not just her boss. She was so easy to talk to and treated everyone with respect. She guessed if she stepped over the line, Meredith would call her on it.

"He calls me every night, just like he said he would. I love having him back in my life and I'm the luckiest girl alive. I have three men who love me, Gramps, Dakota, and my dad."

"You do have a certain glow," she said, emphasizing the word glow. Meredith scowled at her. Changing the subject, Sandra added, "I think the reverend might be a bit smitten with Carrie. What do you think?"

"I think you might be right. He sure has been hanging around here a lot. I hope he'll take it slow though. Carrie could be scared off in a heartbeat."

Sandra agreed. "I know. Her life was terribly tough when Taylor was alive. It's an awful thing to say, but I'm so glad he's not here any longer to hurt her."

Meredith threw some veggies in a bowl and started tossing a salad. "I haven't shed any tears over him, that's for sure. He made my life hell when I was a kid. He was still a sonofabitch after he grew up. Carrie's better off without him."

"Order," Julia yelled. "Three bowls of elk stew."

"I'll get it," Sandra told Meredith.

Meredith's cell phone rang. She wiped her hands on her apron and reached into her purse. "Hello."

"Meredith, how the heck are you?"

"Russ! It's so good to hear from you. What's up?" It was Russell Collins, Meredith's old boss in Florida.

"I have a buyer for your townhome. It's a woman from New York who comes into The Grappling Hook most every day. I can send her to your realtor today if you're interested."

When Meredith first left Florida, she rented her home, not certain whether she was going to stay in Montana or return south. "I'm interested. I have the diner up and running and we're doing a great business. Gramps is getting on in years, so I'm definite about staying on here."

"She's offering you $250,000, cash deal," Russ said excitedly.

"Oh wow, I didn't pay near that when I bought it."

"Well, it's close to the beach, private, and just what she wants. If you want my advice, I'd take the money and run."

"Will I have to come down there for the closing?"

"I'll have your realtor call you after she speaks with the buyer. I'm pretty sure it can be done via phone which will save you a trip."

"That's so great, Russ. Thank you so much for hanging in there with me all this time."

"I kept hoping you'd come back to the Keys. We've all missed you, especially your cooking. I did hire someone part-time to take over until you made up your mind for sure. He knows what he's doing and I'm impressed with him. I think he's going to be very happy when I offer him a full-time position. I kind of figured you wouldn't be coming back."

"Thanks again for everything, Russ. Its noontime here and business is picking up, so I have to let you go. I'll be in touch and you do the same."

"Okay, Sweetie. Good luck to you. I'll take care of everything on this end."

"Great! I owe you one."

The lunch hour was busy and Meredith and Sandra worked steadily during the rush. Taking a break, Meredith sat on a chair thinking over the morning, and how she and Dakota had made love. Going over it in her mind, she was turned on all over again. She couldn't wait for him to get back home. Her thoughts were interrupted when the kitchen door burst open. It was Yuma.

"Something has happened to Dakota!"

CHAPTER THIRTY-FOUR

GRABBING HER JACKET, Meredith rushed out the door with Yuma, nearly tumbling down the stairs in her haste. He gripped her elbow to keep her from falling. "What happened?" she asked breathlessly, trying not to panic. She hurried beside him as fast as she could, aware of the slippery snow. "Where is he? Is he hurt?"

"I'll tell you about it on the way," he said, worry lurking in his eyes. "We must get a move on. He needs us."

"Where's Anna?"

"I picked her up on the way to the diner. She's in the truck. Harry told us Dakota was calling for you."

Cold fear crept into Meredith's body. Calling for her? What did that mean? A trickle of dread washed over her and she could no longer control her emotions. She trembled, tears beginning to fall. "Yuma, please, tell me what happened," she begged.

"Bear got him. That's all I know." Terrified, Yuma dared not speak another word for fear of breaking down. He couldn't lose his only son.

Yuma opened the passenger door and Anna scooted over so Meredith could sit beside her. He closed the door firmly before going around to the other side of the truck and taking a place in the driver's seat.

Meredith gently touched Anna's hand. "Do you know where Dakota is?" *Please God, don't let him die.*

"Livingston Memorial," Anna sniffed, worry in her voice. "It'll be slow going through the pass because of the snow, but we'll make it."

"Do they ever shut the pass down?" Meredith asked, afraid of what the answer might be.

"Sometimes they do," Anna answered, "but I don't think the snowfall is so bad that it'll be shut today."

"I checked with the highway patrol. It's open," Yuma said impatiently.

"It's going to be okay, honey," Anna murmured softly to her husband, placing a loving pat on his knee. "Dakota is strong. Please try not to worry too much until we know what we're up against."

Meredith sat quietly, tears rolling silently down her face, praying that God wouldn't take him from her. A hundred different emotions were running through her body and a knot had formed in her throat making it difficult for her to swallow. She wouldn't allow herself to fall apart in front of Yuma and Anna; they needed her to remain resilient, not a selfish crybaby thinking only of how badly she was feeling. Gently she dabbed her eyes with a Kleenex she'd found wadded up in her jacket pocket.

They made it to Bozeman with little trouble and started their ascent through the pass. The higher they climbed, the faster the snow came down. Yuma snapped on the hazard lights, hoping that if anyone was behind them they'd be more visible.

Drifts began building up along the roadside. The snow and wind lashed unmercifully at the moving vehicle. Visibility was nearly impossible as the wipers worked at a feverish pace to keep the windshield clear. Yuma had a death grip on the steering wheel, his eyes straight ahead. He maneuvered the truck through the deepening snow, steering to the left and to the right, doing everything to keep it from spinning out of control.

Silence filled the vehicle. No one dared to speak. Anna was gripping Meredith's hand, their eyes glued to the road, mentally helping Yuma drive up and down the steep hills. The road seemed to go on forever, both women barely breathing the whole way.

"We're almost there," Yuma muttered, his voice so low they strained to hear what he was saying. "One last hill and that's it. The snow's finally letting up some."

Creeping down the hill, lights from the town came into view guiding them into Livingston. Several minutes later, nerves frazzled, Yuma stopped the truck in front of a convenience store and leaned forward, resting his head on the steering wheel. Exhausted, he moved his head from left to right to loosen the tightness in his neck, and rolled his shoulders forward and backward, releasing some of the tension he felt.

Meredith's hand ached from Anna clutching it so tightly. They'd been certain they would never make it to Livingston alive. She wiggled her fingers back and forth to get rid of the stiffness.

Anna touched Yuma's back gently. "Come on, sweetheart. We need to get to the hospital."

Locating the hospital was easy and soon they were in the parking lot. They ran from the truck into the Emergency area where Harry Goodfellow was waiting for them.

"How's Dakota?" Yuma asked, head throbbing as he put his arm around his wife for support.

"He's in the operating room." Seeing their worried expressions, Harry hurried on explaining, "The bear slapped him around some, so they needed to clean the wounds on his back and suture him up. It was easier to take care of him in there than in the ER."

"Does he have any other injuries?" Anna asked.

"None. He kept his head covered and played dead."

"Where were you when this happened?" Yuma asked suspiciously.

"When Jake caught his scent, we split up. I noticed some bear scat and had my tranquilizer gun ready to take him down." He paused, and went on. "I heard Dakota talking to…I thought he was talking to Jake, when I heard a loud growl. Jake barked, and I went running in their direction."

"What happened next?"

"I heard a loud yelp and when I got to them, Jake was lying in a pool of blood and Dakota was curled up in a ball. The bear was standing over him. I did the only thing I could do. I grabbed my rifle and shot him between the eyes."

"Jake? What about Jake?" Meredith asked, feeling an overwhelming sadness.

"He took one for Dakota." Harry swallowed hard. "He was a great dog, that Jake. I wrapped him in a tarp and put him in our rig. We can bury him when we get home."

Meredith put her hands over her face. The tears she had been holding back all afternoon came rushing forward. Struggling to keep her voice steady, she brushed the tears off her cheeks. "Does Dakota know about Jake?"

"I don't think so," Harry replied. "He probably knows that Jake was hurt, but how bad, I doubt it."

"He's going to be devastated," she said, blinking back the tears.

Anna had said little the whole time, but anger was raging inside her. Meredith, blowing her nose, was unprepared for the onslaught Anna was about to fling at her. "My son nearly lost his life and you're whining about a dog!"

Stunned, Meredith was about to respond to Anna's harsh words, but knew better than to open to her mouth when Anna glared at her with her steely blue eyes. "You have some nerve, waltzing back into town, opening a business, and wrapping my son around your finger. Instead of worrying about him, you're bellyaching about his dog."

Anna caught the stern look Yuma gave her and she said nothing else. Maybe she shouldn't have said anything to Meredith, but she couldn't help herself. The only thing she could think about was how she could have lost her son and all Meredith could talk about was Jake. Anna was usually able to control her emotions, but this time she couldn't. She'd been so afraid. She turned away from Meredith and gave in to her tears, weeping openly.

Yuma put his arms around her and held her until she cried herself out. Whispering in her ear, he said, "You need to pull yourself together before we go see Dakota." What he wanted to say to his wife was that she owed Meredith an apology for her outburst, but thought better of it, given how sensitive Anna had been lately. He decided that this wasn't the time or the place to upset her even more. If he said anything else, he'd be in a no-win situation and he was not a stupid man.

Meredith was speechless over Anna's accusations. She didn't understand why Anna had accused her of not worrying about Dakota. Of course she was worried, she was worried sick, but she knew how he was going to react when he found out his beloved dog was dead. While Meredith was debating about defending her actions, a heavy-set nurse dressed in pink scrubs with tiny horses on them stepped into the waiting area.

"They're bringing Mithter Morgan to hith room now," she lisped, a big smile on her face. "Heth doing well. Come with me and I'll take you to him." They followed the nurse as she waddled down the bluish-grey hallway, her rubber soled shoes making squeaking noises on the tiled floors.

The doctor met them at the door, still in his green surgical scrubs. He shook hands with Yuma and the others before speaking. "Well, he's got some deep gashes on his back which I've stitched up, but other than that he's just fine. He may seem a little drowsy because I gave him a light sedation. I'm keeping him for observation tonight, but you can take him home tomorrow." He moved aside so they could enter the room.

There was no question as to who was going in to see Dakota first. As soon as the doctor gave the green light, Anna hurried into the room, Yuma close on her heels. Dakota was lying on his side, his back covered with sutures and bandages. Hearing footsteps, he groaned as he turned over and tried to sit up.

"You lie still," his mother ordered, straightening his bed sheets. Relieved he looked so well, she gave him a slight cuff to his head, then leaned closer and kissed him on the forehead. "Don't you ever scare me like that again, do you hear?"

Dakota looked at his mother. Her eyes were full of tears. He'd never seen her cry before. "Ma, I'm okay, really. Just a few scratches here and there. I'm going to be fine." He reached up to gently wipe her tears away.

Yuma stood beside his son's bed. Feeling immeasurably better now that he had seen Dakota, he leaned down and gave his son a loving pat on the shoulder. "Do as your mother said. Don't be scaring us again like this," he said gruffly, praying he wouldn't cry in front of his son.

"I won't Father, I promise." He tried sitting up and looked around the room, but the pain made him slump back down onto the bed. "Is Meredith here?"

"She's right outside," Yuma answered. "So is Harry."

"I want to see her. She must have been so frightened. I need to show her that I'm okay." He watched his mother's jaw tighten as she crossed her arms. "What? What's going on here?"

Yuma and Anna looked at each other. "It's nothing," his mother told him. Hand in hand, they left the room. "He wants to see you," Yuma told Meredith.

Before Meredith went in to see Dakota, she felt she needed to say something to Anna. "I'm sorry if I offended you earlier. It wasn't my intent.

Yuma spoke up, not giving Meredith a chance to continue. "We were all caught up in the moment, nerves were frayed, and we were scared Dakota might die. Let's just leave it at that." Yuma glanced at Anna but she added nothing to his comment.

Meredith wanted to give Anna a hug, but knew it wasn't the right time, although she was uncertain why. "Thanks. I love you both and I hope you know I love your son."

"We know you do," Yuma said. Go in and see him now before he tries to get out of bed and come looking for you."

Turning to Harry, Meredith gestured him toward the room. "Why don't you go in first?"

He shook his head. "No you go ahead. I'll be in later. I'm sure he'd rather see your pretty face than my ugly one."

Meredith entered the stark, dimly lit room. She tiptoed over to the bed and peeked at her man. Dakota's eyes were closed, his breathing steady. She was glad he was sleeping considering the ordeal he'd been through. Leaning closer to place a kiss on his cheek, he reached out and grabbed her arm. "Gotcha'!" he chuckled, then groaned when the pain hit him.

She let out an involuntary squeal. "Gosh you scared me, honey. You doing okay?"

"I'm working on it," he said. "Come here, Sweetheart. Crawl up here with me and let me hold you for a minute," he patted the side of the bed.

190

"What about your wounds? You must be in pain."

"I'm fine but I'll be better when you join me." He smiled shamelessly, patting the bed again.

"I don't think I should do this," she replied, climbing up beside him. She snuggled close, careful not to cause him any pain. "You have a one-track mind," she giggled. "Don't forget you're in the hospital."

Dakota wrapped his arms around her. "For a few minutes today, I wondered if I was ever going to see you again." His voice broke and he hugged her more tightly. To hell with the pain.

"I was scared, too. We all were. I'm so grateful you're going to be okay." Leaning up on one arm, Meredith playfully slapped him. "Don't you ever go looking for a bear again," she scolded, laying down and cuddling him again.

"You sound just like my mother," he laughed. "I can see what my life is going to be like having the two of you bossing me around."

Dakota looked at Meredith. Holding her gaze, he placed his lips on hers, kissing her gently at first then more deeply. Their lips fit perfectly together. Their tongues darted in and out like hummingbirds, and he groaned deep down in his throat.

"Whoa there, cowboy," she said, breathlessly, removing his hand from her breast. "I think you need to get some sleep, but before you do, Harry wants to talk to you."

"You sure you don't want to kiss me again?" he grinned, raising his brows.

"I'm not sure of anything when I'm around you," she giggled, getting down from the bed "But anyway, I'm going to get Harry."

She walked to the door and summoned Dakota's friend before returning to the room. She pulled a chair up to the bedside and sat down, dreading the conversation that was about to take place.

Harry walked over to Dakota and shook his hand. "How you doing, pal?"

"I've been better, but the doc says I'm going to be fine. How's Jake?" he asked, concern on his face.

Harry couldn't meet Dakota's questioning eyes. "He…er…he took one for you, Dakota," he answered, swallowing past the lump in his throat. He felt lower than a snake's belly seeing the anguished look on his friend's face.

Meredith grabbed Dakota's hand, but he pushed her away. His hands clenched into fists and he covered his eyes with them. "Oh shit," he moaned. "Why'd he have to die saving my sorry ass?"

Meredith and Harry were struggling to hold it together for Dakota's sake. Loud moans emanating from the room brought his parents and the doctor running in. "What's going on in here?" the doctor demanded.

"He asked about his dog and I had to tell him Jake was dead," Harry explained. "Maybe it wasn't the right time." He'd never seen his friend show this much emotion in all the years he'd known him and wasn't sure how to handle it. Dakota had always been reserved and didn't have much to say, but they'd shared a great friendship just the same. Now he'd gone and broke his friend's heart.

"This just sucks," Harry said, turning and walking out of the room.

CHAPTER THIRTY-FIVE

WEEKS AFTER THE FREAK SNOWSTORM, life was back to normal for the townsfolk of Stony Creek, that is, except for Anna. When Dakota told his mother about his plans of going home with Meredith when he left the hospital, she was very disappointed. For the first time in her life, Anna experienced an unexplained nagging emotion that she couldn't pinpoint.

Maybe it was menopausal. Ever since the feeling had kicked in, she had bouts of the blues, short-tempered outbursts, and crying spells that lasted for days. No matter what the explanation might be, Anna didn't like the way she felt. At first, she tried dismissing her mood swings, but when they persisted, she decided to talk to someone. She picked up the phone and dialed. Hearing her friend's voice, Anna said, "Sadie, it's me. Are you free this afternoon? I really need someone to talk to."

"Well sure, honey. I'm all ears." Sadie knew Anna well enough not to badger her over the phone or she'd clam up and not tell her anything. "How's Dakota doing?" That was a safe subject.

"That's what I want to talk about."

"You come by anytime. I'm here at the store doing inventory. Gage is here, too, so we can go over to my house and have a nice cup of tea or some brandy, whichever you prefer," she laughed.

"I'll be there in about an hour, okay? You better hide the brandy."

"Drive carefully. See you soon." She didn't like the sound of Anna's voice, almost desperate but also sad. What in the world could be making her that upset? She'd know soon enough; in the meantime, Anna had given her reason to worry.

HANGING UP THE PHONE, Anna fixed a cup of tea and sat down at the kitchen table in Charlie's house. She sipped the brown liquid thinking about her duties. In recent years, she had very little to do, but it didn't matter. Every few days she liked to tidy up the place by dusting, running the vacuum, and doing some laundry when Charlie let it pile up. She didn't even have to cook him supper anymore since he started dating Sadie.

She leaned forward, brushing imaginary dust from the table she had just shined. Changing positions, Anna put one foot under her butt letting the other one dangle back and forth. Her thoughts roamed back to when she first met the man who became like a father to her.

She'd been a mere seventeen years old, a white girl and the bride of an eighteen-year-old Black Foot Indian. Ostracized by the town, they were unable to find work. Homeless and starving, Charlie took them under his wing.

That was forty-one years ago. Anna and Yuma lived a good life on the ranch, tending to Charlie, his family and the livestock. She'd even helped raise Meredith when Velvet refused to have much to do with her daughter. Now it was just Charlie since Doris passed away.

Anna recalled how patient, kind, and generous he had been to them. He paid them a decent wage and they gave him a good day's work. Eight years later, when Dakota celebrated his fifth birthday, Charlie deeded them a piece of land and helped them build the home in which they lived to this very day.

As happy as she'd been living on the ranch all these years, suddenly she wanted to run away. She had no control over what was going on in her son's life and she knew that was part of it. For 38 years, she'd watched him grow into a fine man, but now she felt a distance between them, like she didn't know him anymore.

Anna ran her hands through her hair. Why was she feeling like this? She didn't understand it and could find no words to explain the emptiness, the sadness. Talking to Yuma would be fruitless. As much as he loved her, he wouldn't understand. How could she expect him to understand the roller coaster of emotions she was going through when she didn't understand them herself?

Taking the last sip of her tea, she walked over to the sink and rinsed her cup, placing it in the dish rack. She noticed the faucet had a slow drip. She'd have to remind Yuma to fix it. She glanced up at the clock and left.

ANNA PULLED UP IN FRONT of the General Store and went inside, the little bell over the door announcing her arrival. Cupping and rubbing her hands together, she blew gently into them to warm them up. "It's a bit chilly," she said. "I guess I should have worn gloves."

Sadie laid her inventory list on the counter and waved. "Hey there, girlfriend. Glad you're here. I'm ready for some tea, or was that Brandy?" she asked, smiling.

"If I'm wise, I'll have tea and leave it at that." Anna was already feeling a mite better just being in the presence of her friend.

"Gage!" Sadie hollered. The young man came out from the back room, broom in his hand. He was nineteen and looked more like his father, Taylor Boone, every day, something he hated. He was determined never to be like his father, and worked hard at being the opposite of him. "Hi, Miss Morgan," Gage said.

"Hello, Gage. Good to see you. It's been a while."

"Yes, ma'am. Good to see you, too."

"Gage, I'm going home for a little bit. Do you think you can work on this inventory and watch the store, too? " Sadie asked, handing him a clipboard.

"I'm pretty sure I can," he answered. Sadie had shown him how to take inventory several times, but preferred doing it herself. Asking him to take over for her was a huge trust factor. He wouldn't disappoint her.

"Well, we'll be leaving then. I'll be back before closing. You sure you can handle everything?" she asked again, worry lines creasing her brow.

"I'll be fine, Miss Abbott. If I get stuck, I promise to give you a call. How will that be?"

Sadie's face relaxed. "That's great, just what I would want you to do." Sadie and her late husband, Cutter, were never fortunate enough to have children. She'd had an idea lately that she just might leave the General Store to Gage Boone when she was done. He was an upstanding young man, whom she admired so much. He'd never be a good for nothing like his father. "You ready?" she asked Anna.

"Ready. I'll drive. My car's right out front."

The two women walked out into the chilly air. The wind was blowing, as it did ever afternoon, but today it had a nip that made the ladies shiver. "Feels like it could snow," Anna said, looking up at the clouded sky. "Weather forecast is calling for a light dusting," Sadie told her, as they made their way down the boardwalk steps to Anna's car.

"I hope it's not a *light dusting* like the last snow we got," she said sarcastically, remembering the trip through the pass.

Across the street, Doc Elliott was coming out of his office. He waved, turning the OPEN sign to CLOSED, and then locked the door behind him. "Good afternoon, ladies," he said, tipping his hat. "The air's got a bite to it today."

"Afternoon, Doc," they said, agreeing with his assessment of the weather.

"Well, I'm off to the diner for some apple pie and coffee. I have to pick the boys up from school and take them to the dentist in a while."

"Have a scoop of ice cream on that apple pie for me," Sadie grinned.

"I'll remember to do that." Doc flashed a grin back at her. He tipped his hat again and was gone.

The ladies dashed to the car and scurried inside. Anna turned the ignition, cranked up the heater and started down the street. "That doc is a cute one," Sadie shook her head. "I'm surprised no one has snatched him up. He's done a good job raising those boys since Lynda went back east. I heard she divorced him shortly after."

"I can't imagine any woman leaving her children behind," Anna responded. "I hope one of these days Doc will find a mother for his boys, and a good wife for himself."

They turned at the end of Main Street and headed east for a few miles until they came to Dry Run Road where Sadie lived. They made a left turn and headed down the long gravel driveway toward the large two-story farmhouse with wraparound porch.

Sadie and Cutter built the house shortly after they were married with the idea of filling the rooms with the many offspring they hoped to have. Unfortunately, their hopes were crushed when it was discovered Sadie was unable to bear children.

Anna parked in front of the house. They hurried out of the car and ran to open the back door. Dashing inside, the warmth and comfort of Sadie's kitchen welcomed them.

"Brrrrr," Sadie declared, rubbing her palms together. "Sure feels good to get inside. Have a seat, Anna." Sadie grasped the handle of the old teakettle, filled it with water, and put it on the stove to boil.

Anna loved Sadie's vintage kitchen. As modern as hers was, Sadie's was just the opposite. Anna fingered the old crocheted tablecloth, admiring the pineapple pattern someone had so painstakingly worked on. "This is beautiful," she told Sadie.

"I love it. I bought it at a yard sale a few years ago for a dollar. Can you imagine that?" She reached into the cupboard for a teapot, two cups and saucers and set them on the sideboard until the water was hot. "Would you like a muffin?" she asked Anna, passing her a napkin.

"No thanks. I just need to talk."

"What's on your mind?" Sadie asked, pulling out a chair and sitting beside her. "You look miserable and you've had me worried."

"I feel like such a jerk and so selfish," Anna told her. "Ever since Dakota went home from the hospital with Meredith, I've been stewing about it."

"He's going to be okay, isn't he?"

"He's fine. I'm the one who isn't. I've been in such a cranky mood I can't stand myself." She looked at Sadie, hoping she'd understand. "*I* wanted him to come home with his father and me. *I* wanted to take care of him and he went home with HER!"

The teakettle whistled. "Hold that thought," Sadie said as she got up and turned off the stove. She hurried back to the table. "Why are you so mad at Meredith?"

"I don't *know*." Anna burst into tears.

"Oh honey," Sadie murmured, putting her arms around Anna and giving her a big squeeze. "Don't get mad at what I'm about to say, but I think you're experiencing a bit of jealousy."

Anna pulled away, as if she'd been stung by a bee. "I've never heard of anything so foolish in my whole life. Dakota's been in love with Meredith for as long I can remember and it's never bothered me."

Sadie got up and went to the counter, glancing over her shoulder at Anna before she spoke. "She was never a threat, until now."

"What's that supposed to mean?" Anna barked.

"Meredith left home at eighteen and has been gone for twenty years. Dakota has been yours all this time, dating here and there but nothing serious, nothing for you to get all fussed up about."

Sadie placed the cups and saucers on the table and poured the boiling water onto the teabags. Taking her place next to Anna, she dunked her teabag up and down in the hot liquid while she continued. "Now she's back and you're seeing less and less of your son. When Dakota was in the hospital, it was Meredith he called for, not his mother. I'll bet that stung," she said, eyeing Anna. "As much as he loves you, his love for Meredith is completely different. He may be thirty-eight years old, but I think you're suffering from the empty nest syndrome, my friend."

"Oh for heaven's sake." Disgusted, Anna stood up and threw her napkin onto the table. "Have you completely lost your mind?"

"I don't think so. You need to dig deep, Anna, and see what's really going on. Once you do, I think you're going to feel a whole lot better."

Anna slumped back down into the chair. "Do you really think I'm jealous?" It was hard for her to imagine. She'd never been jealous of anyone a day in her life. On second thought, maybe she never had a cause to feel that way she reasoned.

"Do you want a muffin now?" Sadie coaxed, a big grin on her face. "A good muffin and a cup of hot tea can soothe the soul." A loud growl rumbled from Sadie's stomach. "I guess I could use one myself."

Anna laughed. "I haven't eaten much in the past few days. Did Meredith make these?"

"She sure did. I bought six of them this morning when I stopped in to see Charlie before opening the store. Lately he goes there for breakfast. He loves having Meredith home and is proud of how well she's doing."

"I feel like such a shit," Anna said remorsefully. "I haven't been very nice to her at all. I haven't even gone to work the past couple of weeks. I know Sandra is cooking with her, so I figured she didn't need me anyway."

"Well, you've been having a regular old pity party lately, huh? Someone not only steals your son, someone else steals your job. Ungrateful bastards!"

"Sadie!"

Sadie chuckled. "See how ridiculous it all is when you put it in perspective." She reached for Anna's hand and squeezed it lovingly. "Your life, as you knew it, has been turned upside down these past few months. It's a wonder you didn't go off the deep end before now," she said, her eyes dancing in amusement.

"I did not go off the deep end, although Yuma and Charlie would probably argue the point. They think I'm nuts and walk a wide path around me." Anna started to laugh. "Poor guys, I've been horrible to live with."

"Have you seen Dakota since he's been home?"

"I wasn't about to go to Meredith's house. As much as I wanted to see my son, I expected that he would come to see me. That didn't happen, so finally I called him. He got angry and told me that when I came to my senses, we could talk."

"Did you tell him how you were feeling?"

"I did. I told him I thought this thing with Meredith was moving much too fast and he needed to come home."

"I bet that went over like a fart in church," Sadie muttered, rolling her eyes.

"It did. He was furious and said I was treating him like a teenager, not a grown man able to make his own decisions. Then he did the unthinkable…he hung up on me!"

"What a brat! He needs to be horsewhipped, that's what!" Both women burst out laughing. "I wonder who'd hold him down?" Sadie roared.

"He'd probably drop on all fours if Meredith sashayed by, then we'd get him," Anna let out another hearty laugh. "Oh Sadie, seriously, thanks so much for listening to me. I can't believe I was feeling so terrible because I didn't want to lose my baby boy. I do love Meredith, I always have. I guess I felt like she was taking my place when that's not the case at all.

"No one will ever take your place in Dakota's life, Anna. You're his mother and always will be. You have a special bond that will last through the sands of time. Now give me a big hug and let's get out of here. I have to get back to the store."

Walking out to the car, Anna was thankful for the wonderful friendship she shared with Sadie. She felt that all was right in her world now. She knew she had a lot of explaining to do and apologies to make. She hoped it wasn't too late.

CHAPTER THIRTY-SIX

TRIPP SEARCHED FOR HIS FRIEND for days, nose to the ground, desperate to pick up Jake's scent. He'd be gone for hours. Meredith would hear him in the distance, howling, calling for his pal who could no longer hear him. The lonely little collie would come home, flop on the floor, put his head on his paws, and sigh, very loud sighs that broke Meredith's heart. He didn't want to eat, but would take a few bites to please his mistress when she hand fed him. Meredith was afraid he might die from loneliness and knew she had to do something. She needed to find a job for Tripp.

Dakota, on the other hand, wasn't much better. His wounds had healed, but he hadn't returned to work. He moped around the house, saying little, and the look on his face was so sad it moved Meredith to tears. He not only lost his faithful companion, he'd had a huge fight with his mother which hadn't been resolved. She knew it was tearing him up inside, but both he and Anna were stubborn. Neither one was going to give.

The doorbell rang, startling her. Not expecting company, she fluffed up her hair with her fingers and hurried to open the door. Anna was standing on the porch, a basketful of muffins and a huckleberry pie in her hands. "Anna. What a wonderful surprise. Come in. Come in." *Good Lord, I wonder what's going to happen now.*

"Is Dakota home? I need to talk to both of you" Her chin wobbled. *I will not cry!*

"He's upstairs taking a nap. Please, come in out of the cold. There's some fresh coffee in the kitchen. I'll go wake Dakota."

She's being so nice to me after I've been such a shit. I figured I'd get the door slammed in my face, and she's inviting me in for coffee. Anna went to the kitchen and set the pie and muffins on the counter. Knowing Meredith's house as well as she knew her own, she opened the cupboard, took out three coffee mugs, and placed them on the table. Then she sat, waiting for them to come downstairs.

Tripp got up from his rug, stretched, and ambled over to Anna. He looked up at her with woeful eyes, let out a small whine, and laid his head on her lap. "Poor little guy. You're missing your friend, aren't you?" She leaned forward and nuzzled his neck. He licked her hand. "You're welcome," she whispered, patting him on the head.

Meredith jostled Dakota. Instinctively, he reached for her. "Your mother is here. She wants to talk to both of us."

Dakota turned over and looked at Meredith. "I don't know if I want to listen to what she has to say."

"Look, this has been going on long enough," she admonished. "The holidays are coming up and I'm not going to have a family rift spoiling mine, get it?" She poked him in the chest with her finger, turned on her heel and stomped loudly down the stairs.

"He'll be down in a few minutes," she told Anna. "How about I pour us each a cup of coffee while we're waiting? I'd love one of those muffins, too. You want one?"

"None for me thanks, but I will have coffee." Anna was nervous. Would Dakota come down stairs and let her apologize?

If he chose not to, she'd apologize to Meredith anyway. "So how have you been?"

"I've been okay. We're busy at the diner. I hope you're going to come back one of these days. I need you and I miss you, too." Meredith set the mugs of coffee in front of them. "Things around here have been a bit iffy. Tripp is a mess and so is Dakota. They miss Jake so much."

At the mention of Jake's name, Tripp's head jerked up from Anna's lap, hope in his eyes. "Sorry little buddy," Meredith soothed, reaching out to stroke his head. "God, this is so sad."

"What's so sad?" The husky male voice made the women look up. Dakota was standing in the doorway, arms crossed rebelliously, ready for a fight. His long black hair, usually pulled back in a ponytail, was hanging loosely and fell across his shoulders down onto his chest.

He is so damn hot, hotter than hot. Meredith's brain turned mushy every time she saw Dakota, especially now that she'd seen him naked.

"Um, I was just telling your mother it's so sad how much Tripp is missing Jake."

"We all miss Jake," he snarled. "Why are you here?" he asked, giving his chin a jerk toward Anna.

I might just as well come right out with it. She drew in a deep breath, "I came to apologize." *There it's out. What's he going to do now?*

"Dakota, please sit down." Meredith patted the chair next to her. "Your mother came all the way out here and you should listen to what she has to say."

"Oh yeah, like she did the last time we spoke?" he snorted. He remained standing.

"Well, I'm going to say what I came to tell you and then

I'll leave." Anna wanted to stand up and face them, but she was afraid her legs would buckle under her so she stayed put. "It's hard for me to admit, but I was jealous of Meredith."

Meredith's jaw dropped open. She was about to speak when Anna put her finger up, shushing her.

"I never thought I could be jealous of anyone, but I had all these emotions roiling inside of me that I didn't understand. I lashed out at everyone I cared about." She let out a little laugh. "It's a wonder I still have a husband. Thank God he loves me because living with me these last several weeks has been awful."

Dakota stepped into the kitchen. "Ma..."

"Let me finish. I was so scared when the bear got you and we didn't know whether you'd live or die, at least not until we got to the hospital. You looked so pathetic, all bandaged up like that. I wanted you to come home with us, but you chose to go to Meredith's. That irritated me so much. I guess that's where the jealousy came in, although I didn't know what it was at the time." She hesitated before going on. "I stewed over your decision and decided it was all Meredith's fault. Then you and I had the phone conversation," she looked at her son, "and I told you I thought it was too soon to get serious over someone who might up and leave again. That's about the time you hung up on me."

Dakota thought for a minute before speaking. "I'm all grown up, Ma. I don't need you taking care of me anymore, not that I haven't appreciated it in the past. My life is different now, can't you understand that?"

"I know. I overstepped my bounds and said some mean, hurtful things, all because I felt like I was losing you." She couldn't stop the tears any more than she could stop her heart from beating.

Dakota walked across the room and kneeled in front of his mother. "You're never going to lose me, silly woman.

You're my ma and I love you." He rubbed his mother's hands between his own. This was the second time in his life that he watched her cry, both times because of him. "Ma, stop crying and listen to me."

Anna sniffled and swiped at the tears streaming down her face. Meredith passed her a box of Kleenex.

"I owe you an apology, too. I was grief-stricken over Jake. I felt so guilty that he was dead because of me. I should have taken care of him, instead of the other way around. When you called and started reaming me out about Meredith, I just snapped. You bore the brunt of all my anguish and for that, I'm truly sorry."

He reached for his mother and put his arms around her. Holding onto him tightly, she sobbed. He tenderly patted her back, murmuring words only she could hear. When she'd regained her composure, she sat back on the chair and blew her nose. "I think I'll have another cup of coffee now if it's okay."

Meredith scurried across the kitchen to grab the coffee pot. Pouring a cup for Anna, she refilled hers and asked Dakota if he wanted some.

"Meredith, I guess you know how sorry I am, but I need to say it. I'm terribly sorry for being such a shrew, and I'd love to come back to the diner if you'll have me."

Meredith hugged Anna. "I accept your apology, although I don't think one is necessary. You did what any mother would do under the same circumstances. I acted like a half-wit at the hospital so it's no wonder you were upset with me. As far as the diner, I can't wait for you to come back. No one likes *my* muffins. They all want to know when Anna is coming back."

She smiled at the woman who had loved her like a daughter for most of her life. "Now that that's over with, I think we need to discuss Thanksgiving and Christmas. We don't have much time. I'm so excited to be spending the holidays with my family for the first time years."

Dakota took Tripp for a walk while the two women spent the rest of the afternoon making plans for the upcoming festivities. They called Sadie who agreed to come over and help.

REMEMBERING TRIPP'S SULLENNESS, Meredith made a phone call to Jethro Byrd, a neighboring rancher. She'd heard he and his crew planned to move cattle from the range closer to his ranch in a few days. She dialed his number. He answered on the third ring.

"Jethro, here."

"Hi, Jethro, it's Meredith Banning. I heard you're going to be moving some cattle in a couple of days and wondered if you could help me out."

"Yup, want to get them closer before the heavy snow comes. What can I do for ya?"

"Well, I suppose you heard about Dakota's shepherd getting killed."

"I did. Damn shame, too. He was a good dog."

"My dog, Tripp, has been pining around ever since. I was wondering if you could take him with you. He needs to work, something to get his mind off losing his friend."

"Happy to do it," Jethro told her. "Bring him by the night before. He can sleep in the barn with the rest of the dogs. They've all met each other so it should be okay. I'll give you a call and let you know when."

"Thanks so much. I hope this will be just the thing to get my young dog back on track. I'll see you soon." She hung up the phone and called to Tripp.

"Hey fella, you want to go on a cattle drive?"

He whined and laid his head in Meredith's lap.

Stony Creek Diner

    "Oh come on. It'll be good for you, just you wait and see." She patted the little collie's fur and gave him a hug. "Everything is going to be okay, Tripp." Meredith had a plan.

CHAPTER THIRTY-SEVEN

AFTER MUCH DISCUSSION, Sadie opted to host Thanksgiving dinner at her house, breaking with tradition of having the meal at Charlie's. Meredith and Anna agreed to help with the cooking. They decided to keep the occasion small, only family, being that this was their first holiday together in many years. Dallas would be on the road, but promised Meredith he'd be home before New Year's Eve.

The day before Thanksgiving, the three women gathered to cook and help Sadie set the table. They made pies, cookies, bread, stuffing, and cranberry Jell-O salad, Charlie's favorite. Sadie's vintage refrigerator was too small to hold much, but fortunately, she kept her modern French door fridge on the back porch. Cutter bought it for her just before he passed away and she didn't have the heart to get rid of it. The ladies filled the shelves with condiments and the turkey, which Sadie planned to stuff and cook bright and early the next morning.

"Whew," Sadie said, pulling out a chair and flopping down into it. "Have a seat, ladies. I forgot how much work went into preparing a big meal like this."

Anna and Meredith followed suit. "Is anyone thirsty?" Meredith asked. "I sure could use a nice cold drink of that lemonade we just made. How about it?"

"I'll have a glass," Anna said. "Sadie?

"Sounds good."

The women discussed the upcoming annual Stony Creek Cowboy Christmas Ball, an event where everyone from miles around attended. "The ball is only four weeks away," Sadie chimed in. "Charlie and his committee have been working on it for nearly a year. It's going to be a wonderful time."

"I don't remember there being a Christmas ball when I was a young girl," Meredith said.

"I think the first ball was about fifteen years ago. Wouldn't that be right, Anna?

"Sounds about right," Anna replied.

Sadie stretched her arms, rolled her shoulders, and pushed back from the table. She was tired. "Let's go set the table so we'll be done for the day. I think I could use a catnap."

THANKSGIVING DAY BLEW IN blustery and cold. The early snowfall had stripped the aspens and cottonwoods of their vibrant yellow colors and foliage. Everyone said it was going to be a long, hard winter.

Meredith and Dakota arrived at Sadie's a couple of hours before dinner, so Meredith could help her in the kitchen. Anna and Yuma showed up shortly after with the same idea in mind. Charlie was already there having spent the night with Sadie.

"Mmmm, the house smells wonderful." Meredith sniffed in the delicious aroma. The women went directly to the kitchen; the men gathered in the living room to watch the Macy's Parade and to stay out from underfoot. The less seen, the less they'd be called on to do.

An hour later Sadie called from the dining room, "Come and get it." The men hurried from their chairs, mouths watering in anticipation of the fine cooking they were about to partake of. "Table looks pretty," Charlie told Sadie, putting an arm around her shoulder.

A white tablecloth with colorful autumn leaves around the edges covered the long wooden table. The centerpiece was a large white candle in a clear cylinder adorned with several ears of Indian corn secured with twine. Acorns bound with wire and twisted into a loop held the bright orange napkins. Handmade place cards with small pieces of bittersweet glued to their corners were placed next to the napkins.

"Thanks, honey. I wanted everything to look perfect. I'll bet there isn't a prettier table in all of Gallatin County, if I do say so myself. Okay everyone, please find your seat and let's get started."

Meredith looked at her family and the men who loved her so much. She had so much to be thankful for this Thanksgiving Day. Her heart was overflowing with happiness and tears welled up in her eyes.

"Hey," Dakota nudged her. "What's wrong?"

"There's not a thing wrong," she whispered. "It's just that I haven't been this happy in my whole life. I forgot what it feels like to be part of something."

"We're all together now, and that's the way we're going to stay." He squeezed her hand and smiled.

"I think it's time we gave thanks to the good Lord for this wonderful day," Sadie said, holding out her hand to Charlie, who did the same to Meredith and on it went around the table. "Let's bow our heads in prayer and then we'll go around the table and each one of us can say what we're most thankful for." She heard a few soft groans but ignored them.

"Dear Heavenly Father, Thank You for this special day, a day to remember Your goodness to us. Thank You for a roof over our heads, and more than enough food to eat. Thank You for the family and friends You have given to us, who have gathered together to eat this Thanksgiving Day meal. Amen."

"Now let's see what everyone is thankful for. Anna, we'll start with you."

"I'm thankful that my son is alive, well, and happy and for my wonderful husband who has put up with me these past couple of months. Yuma?"

"I, too, am thankful that my son is alive and well, and that my wife is back to her old self." Yuma smiled at Anna and hugged her. "Dakota, you're next."

"I'm thankful that Meredith is back in my life. I've loved her for as long as I can remember and now she's here with me. I'm thankful for wonderful parents who only want the best for me. Oh yeah, I'm thankful I wasn't the bear's dinner. Meredith?"

Meredith patted Dakota's knee and grinned at him. "I'm thankful to be back in Stony Creek with my family and with the man who's waited for me to wake up and realize how much he means to me. I'm thankful to Velvet for buying the diner, even though I thought she was crazy when I first saw it. I'm thankful to each of you who have welcomed me home unconditionally. Gramps?"

Charlie sniffled, and pulled a handkerchief out of his back pocket. He wiped his tears before speaking. "Now you've gone and made an old man cry."

"Sorry, Gramps."

"Well, I'm grateful to have my granddaughter home at last." He looked over at Sadie and took her hand. "I'm so very grateful that this little woman has overlooked all my faults and loves me anyway. I never thought I'd be this happy again."

"Oh, Charlie. I feel the same way. I never thought love would come my way again, but God knew we would find each other. For that, I'm most thankful. I think it's time to eat. Charlie would you come out to the kitchen with me and bring in the turkey?"

"I'd be happy to. Don't know about the rest of you, but I'm starving."

CHAPTER THIRTY-EIGHT

DECEMBER BROUGHT MILDER TEMPERATURES and most of the snow on the ground had melted. Tripp was back from his round up, energized and fulfilled. Jethro commented that he was a natural and could use him again on another drive. Meredith, willing to do anything that would make her collie happy, agreed.

Planning the Christmas Ball took most of Charlie's and the committee's time. They scheduled the ball for December 21st, 7pm, at Buckshill State Park's large recreation hall.

"I called Jeff Hinsman yesterday, you know the guy who's the lead of the Big Sky Brothers Band, and asked him if they'd perform at the ball. He said he'd be happy to help out and looked forward to it," Howard Jasper told the men.

"Good. We can scratch that off the list," Charlie replied.

The Christmas Ball appealed to all ages, especially the children who waited in excited anticipation to see Santa Claus.

"Are we going to ask everyone to dress in western attire this year?" George Logan asked. "Last time the men wore shirts, vests, and jeans and the ladies wore skirts and blouses. They sure did look pretty, the ladies that is."

The men laughed. Jigger Johnson spoke up. "I think that's a good idea. Last year the local women prepared a potluck dinner and it went over well. Suppose we dare ask them again? It's a lot of work."

"We can toss the idea out there and see what response we get. If they don't want to do it, then we'll ask anyone attending to bring something to share. By the way, no alcohol either," Charlie said.

In past years, drunkenness had been an issue, so to avoid the problem, alcohol was prohibited. The men agreed.

Once the plans were in place, they passed the word to the local women, knowing that the information would get to each household quicker through them than sending an email.

MEREDITH ROSE EARLY THE DAY before the ball. She intended to make a trip over to Bozeman to pick up a special gift for Dakota.

WHEN MEREDITH AND DAKOTA ARRIVED at the ball, they were amazed to find the hall simply but beautifully decorated, with a huge Christmas tree in one corner.

The women decided that every family attending should bring a dish. That would take the pressure off the town's ladies, and food should be plentiful. The band was playing Christmas carols and people were milling around greeting each other.

Meredith was dressed in a bright red skirt, plaid blouse in Christmas colors, and black boots. Her hair fell in soft curls around her face. Dakota had a difficult time from running his fingers through her beautiful locks.

He was dressed in black jeans, red shirt, black vest and bolo tie. His black mane was pulled back and secured with a small piece of leather. Meredith thought he never looked more handsome.

Charlie, Sadie, Yuma and Anna would join them shortly. Meredith and Dakota found a table large enough to hold the six of them and sat down. Linda and Larry Owens stopped by to wish them a Merry Christmas.

"Sure nice to see you doing so well, Dakota," Larry said. "You gave us all a scare."

"Thanks, Larry. I'm fine. Merry Christmas."

"Is Carrie coming?" Meredith asked.

"She sure is," Linda said with a big grin on her face. "I'm not supposed to say a word, but I can't help myself. Reverend Anderson is her date for the evening."

"I thought I saw a spark between them a while back. Good for her. She couldn't find a nicer guy, except for Dakota here," she teased, nudging him in the ribs.

"Don't say I told you. She'd skin me alive."

"Your secret is safe with me. Hope to see you later on."

Dakota shook his head. "You women couldn't keep a secret if your lives depended on it."

"You'd be surprised." She thought about the secret she was keeping from Dakota. *He'll be eating those words soon enough,* she thought, the corners of her mouth turning up into a slight smile.

"Here you are," Sadie said, taking a seat next to Meredith. "Your grandpa is parking the truck. Sure wish he'd get rid of that old thing. Those springs sticking through the upholstery are going to give me lockjaw. We're going to have a come-to-Jesus understanding pretty soon; the truck or me."

Meredith laughed aloud, picturing in her mind how that would play out. "I love your skirt. You look amazing, tonight."

"Oh, this old thing," Sadie protested, skimming her fingers over the black velvet skirt she was wearing.

"It's beautiful and so are you. Your blouse is lovely, too."

Sadie was wearing a long-sleeved white, silk blouse with a yoke collar, a cameo brooch nestled between the V in the neckline. Baby's breath adorned her long hair, pulled into a fashionable up do. Her green eyes sparkled and her cheeks appeared to be flushed, almost as if she had a secret of her own.

"Here comes Charlie now." She flashed him a big grin, and he leaned down to kiss her on the cheek.

"Gramps, you sure do clean up nice." Charlie was wearing black jeans and boots, a white shirt with a bow tie, and a black vest. His pure white hair accented his outfit and he looked as handsome as any cowboy could.

"Thanks, sweetheart." He looked around the room, happy to see such a large turnout. "Guess all our hard work paid off."

"This is wonderful, Gramps. To think I've missed out on all of this simply because my feelings were hurt and I was being stubborn."

Sadie spotted Carrie and the reverend making their way to the table. "Meredith, don't look now but here comes Carrie and her date."

"Hello everyone," Carrie greeted her friends, blushing as the reverend took her hand.

"Glad to see you all." It was obvious that he was smitten with Carrie. He'd been patient waiting for her to agree to date him.

Anna and Yuma arrived, apologizing for being late. Ever since she'd made peace with her son, her husband, and Meredith, she was a totally different person. Her love for Yuma was more than she could express, and lately she couldn't keep her hands off him. He didn't object when Anna wanted a romp in the hay before the dance. Hell, he would have spent the night at home if she'd wanted to. They were giddy as two teenagers and didn't fool anyone.

The ball was in full swing by 8pm. The band had kicked into country music and the dance floor was crowded with everyone from children to adults, dancing the country two-step, country waltz, and line dancing.

"Hold on!" Jeff Hinsman hollered into his microphone. The dancers stopped and looked at him. "What's that I hear? Jingle bells?"

The children started screaming and running toward the door. "Santa's coming," they cried out.

Flinging the door open, Santa emerged with a huge sack slung over his back, full of gifts for the little ones. "Ho, Ho, Ho," he chuckled, stomping across the room to the Christmas tree. Pillows stuffed inside his red pants gave him an ample belly and a fake white beard covered his face. He took a seat in a big, plush green chair, setting his bag down.

The children knelt on the floor in front of him, watching carefully as he pulled out the first gift. Each child, called by name, was given a present appropriate for them. The children's names were given to Sadie weeks earlier, so that no child would be left out.

There was one gift left, a big green box hidden behind the tree, tied with a bright, red bow. "Hmmm," Santa mused. "I wonder who this belongs to?" He made a big production getting the tag off the box and holding it out in front of him, pretending not to be able to read it. "What's this say?" he squinted through his tiny little spectacles.

"Tell us who it's for, Santa," the children chimed. "Tell us, Santa."

"I think it says, but it couldn't be, could it?'

"What Santa, what?"

"It says Dakota Morgan! Dakota, you come on down here."

Dakota didn't move a muscle, paralyzed when he heard his name called. *This must be some kind of joke.*

"Go on, Dakota," Anna said, giving him a little shove. "Go see what Santa has for you." She didn't know what the gift was either and was just as intrigued as the rest of them.

Dakota, duly embarrassed, begrudgingly rose from his chair and walked across the room. Everyone was rooting him on.

"I need some help with this box," Santa told him. "It's quite heavy."

Dakota leaned down to pick up the box. It moved. *What the hell?* He pulled the box out from under the tree and it moved a second time, a small whine coming from inside the package.

His heart lurched at the sound. With shaking hands, he untied the ribbon. Just as he was about to take the cover off, a small ball of black and tan fur wriggled out of the box and fell onto his lap. Dakota's breath caught. Carefully he picked up the tiny Shepard puppy who rewarded him with kisses on his face and hands. The crowd cheered, knowing how sad he'd been after losing Jake.

"Well, folks, that's it for Santa this year. Oh, not to worry kiddies. Santa will be coming to your house in a few more days. Oh, one more thing. Is Meredith Banning here?"

Meredith looked over at her grandfather. He shrugged his shoulders.

She stood up, all eyes were on her.

"Come on down here and give old Santa a hug, little girl."

Meredith's face broke into a welcoming smile as she ran toward Santa and threw her arms around him. "Merry Christmas, Daddy."

Dallas harumped, trying to remain composed. "Best you two get back to your table so we can get on with the festivities. I gotta' go change."

Dakota was still speechless. What a night this had been. He stood up, hugging the tiny dog to his chest. Meredith joined him and they walked back to the table together. Anna and Sadie wiped tears from their eyes.

"You want to take it back?" Meredith jeered, taking her seat.

"Take what back?"

"You want to take it back that women can never keep a secret? I think I just proved how very wrong you are."

"Your dad and gramps kept an awesome secret, too, it seems." He sat down beside her and leaned over to give her a deep kiss, the pup wiggling between them. "I love you. Thank you so much. This is one of the best gifts I've ever received."

"I love you, too. He needs a name. I'm glad you're happy. I was afraid you wouldn't want another dog right now, but I was willing to take the chance. I can't wait until Tripp sees him."

Dallas changed out of his Santa suit and dressed in appropriate getup joined them at the table.

"Ladies and gentlemen," Jeff Hinsman said, tapping on the microphone. The crowd went silent waiting to hear what Jeff had to propose. "Reverend Anderson. Would you please come up on the stage?"

Storm Anderson, handsome in his cowboy attire, excused himself from Carrie and strode onto the platform. "Hi folks. Well, we have another big surprise in store for you tonight. Sadie and Charlie, would you please come forward."

Meredith and Dakota stared at each other in shock. What was going on? Sadie, Charlie, Anna and Yuma all stood and walked toward the stage.

"Folks, we are about to have a wedding!" the reverend shouted. The crowd roared. "Charlie, Sadie, please step forward. Anna, you stand beside Sadie, and Yuma, you get over there beside Charlie. Charlie and Sadie please face each other and join hands." Reverend Anderson stepped down to stand before them.

Meredith held fiercely onto Dakota's hand and tried to hold back her tears. Talk about keeping secrets! She was going to kick her granddad in the butt for not letting her in on the plan.

"Dear friends. Love is the reason we are here at this hour, to witness and to celebrate the joining of two separate lives. In marriage we not only say, 'I love you today,' but also, 'I promise to love you all of our tomorrows.' Charles and Sadie, in the days ahead of you, there will be stormy times and good times, times of conflict and times of joy. I ask you to remember this advice:

Never go to bed angry.

Let your love be stronger than your anger.

Learn the wisdom of compromise, for it is better to bend than to break.

Believe the best of your beloved rather than the worst.

Confide in your partner and ask for help when you need it.

Remember that true friendship is the basis for any lasting marriage.

Give your spouse the same courtesies and kindnesses you bestow on your friends.

Say, 'I love you' every day."

The reverend went on. "Charles and Sadie have written their own vows. Sadie, you may go first."

Sadie's hands were shaking and Charlie squeezed them tightly for encouragement. "Charlie, because of you, I laugh, I smile, I dare to dream again. I look forward with great joy to spending the rest of my life with you, caring for you, nurturing you, being there for you in all life has for us. I vow to be true and faithful for as long as we both shall live."

Charlie swallowed hard hearing the loving words spoken to him by his bride to be. He hoped he could measure up to what she thought he was. "Sadie, my darlin', you are my best friend.

221

Today I give myself to you in marriage. I promise to encourage and inspire you, to laugh with you, and to comfort you in times of sorrow and struggle. I promise to love you in good times and in bad, when life seems easy and when it seems hard. I promise to cherish you, and to always hold you in highest regard. These things I give to you today, and all the days of our life."

"Wow," Sadie whispered. Never had she felt so loved. Charlie reached out and gently wiped a tear from her cheek.

"The rings, please."

Anna and Yuma passed the wedding rings they had been clutching to the reverend.

The reverend held up the two rings. "The wedding ring is the outward and visible sign of an inward and spiritual bond which unites two loyal hearts in endless love. It is a seal of the vows Charles and Sadie have made to one another. Bless O God these rings that Charles and Sadie, who give them, and who wear them, may ever abide in thy peace, living together in unity, love and happiness for the rest of their lives. Charles, place the ring on Sadie's finger, and Sadie please do the same for Charles."

With the rings exchanged, the reverend proceeded. "In as much as you have pledged your love and devotion to one another, by the power vested in me by the great State of Montana, I pronounce you husband and wife. Charlie, you may kiss your bride."

"Now I gotcha," Charlie said, eyes twinkling as he pulled Sadie to him and planted a firm kiss on his new wife.

"Folks, please welcome for the first time, Charlie and Sadie Parker!"

When Charlie and Sadie turned to greet their guests, the band struck up *Forever and Ever, Amen*, amidst clapping, cheering, and foot stomping.

Meredith ran over to her grandfather and Sadie and hugged them. "I was crowing about how well I could keep a secret, and here the two of you were planning a wedding. That's a whopping secret to keep. I can't believe you pulled it off." She grinned at her granddad. "You old devil, you. I didn't know you were such a romantic."

"There's a lot of things you don't know about your grandfather," Sadie snickered. Charlie turned a fine shade of red.

Friends gathered around to shake hands and give hugs to the new bride and groom. There hadn't been a wedding in Stony Creek for quite a while. What a gift the town received this Christmas.

MEREDITH LOOKED AT THE PUPPY, asleep in Dakota's arms. "Do you think it's time we took this little guy home?"

"I do, but before we go there's something I need to say to you."

Puzzled, she looked at him.

"I love you and I'll always love you, you know that, right?"

She nodded. Her stomach was doing flip-flops. What was he trying to say? Did the excitement of the evening push him into realizing he wasn't ready for a long-term relationship with her?

Seeing the confused look on her face, and the fear in her eyes, Dakota struggled on. "Meredith, I want to marry you if you'll have me."

Relief washed over her. She threw her arms around Dakota, squeezing him and the puppy. "Of course I'll marry you," she murmured. "Let's not say anything tonight though. I think Stony Creek has had enough surprises for one day and we don't want to take away the shine from Gramps and Sadie's big day."

"Sounds good to me." Dakota put his arm around Meredith's waist. They grabbed their coats and headed out the door. "We'll share our own surprise on New Year's Eve."

Stony Creek Diner

ABOUT THE AUTHOR

Sharon Allen is a native of Maine. She and her husband, Gordon (Bud), moved to Florida in 2005. They will celebrate their 10th anniversary in November.

Sharon has four children, four grandchildren, two great grandchildren, and a Scottish terrier, Duffy.

She is a member of The Red Hat Society and is Queen of her chapter. She belongs to the Florida Writers Association, Writers League of The Villages, The Write Corner, and Romance Writers of America. She loves photography.

For more information about Sharon, you can visit her website: sharonallenauthor.com

Stony Creek Diner